Reconnecting Cities, People, and Nature
Exercises in Urban Design

Birkhäuser

Víctor Muñoz Sanz and Robbert Jan van der Veen

Foreword

Rahul Mehrotra

Reconnecting Cities, People, and Nature: Exercises in Urban Design stimulates us to reinstill common sense in our work molding the built environment as urban designers and critical actors. It leads us to radical ideas while at the same time reinforcing obvious readings of urban design and its instrumentality as a practice in today's world. The argument presented here reminds us that urban design is a bridge practice, which implies flow and openness. It is a flexible practice that reconfigures itself depending on the problem and the agents, actors, and constituencies it must influence. Flexible enough to configure and reconfigure itself between built form and the broader ecologies of the natural and social ecosystems within which it is situated. Most importantly, this book commits us to broadening the material reality that urban design deals with in order to unequivocally embrace the natural and social ecosystems that are the foundation upon which we build. This implies that we must renounce our business-as-usual rhetoric by embracing the modesty of the light and reversible and becoming more centered around the equitable relationship between humankind and natural environment that humans have so severely degraded, at great cost to our own future as a species. We must commit to the simultaneous validity of modes of engagement as well as to the transgressions and synergies between disparate disciplinary cultures, modes of representation, knowledge accumulation, and production. It means walking the razor-thin line between the often-polarized imaginaries of time that inform the making of urban design and its usefulness in perpetuity versus its transitionary purpose. This imagined binary requires unsettling and challenging the relevance of the static permanent manifestation of urban design and by extension architecture as the singular spectacle or organizing instrument of the city.

Today, this sense of disengagement with the broader and more encompassing reality has attracted criticism of what urban design has come to mean. The many forms and readings of "urbanism" emerging around us really serve as a critique of the unrealized potential of urban design to engage in site creation in more substantial ways. And it is ironic that urban design as a practice is intrinsically concerned with the spatial implications of urban aspirations, cultures, politics, and so on. The definition of urban design in addition to its active dimension of closing the feedback loops between city planning, landscape, and architecture, is necessarily explicitly human and nature-centric. In fact, urban design is about activism, about drawing the disciplines of architecture, landscape, and urban planning closer together and being a conduit for the critical feedback loops upon which the survival and improvement of our cities and broader landscapes depend! The structure of this book and the arguments highlighted in the 20 exercises is a wonderful series of unfolding provocations that carries us through various topics at different scales and in frameworks of various complexity. These exercises are like illustrations and designed to trigger new spatial, strategic, and representative imaginaries. Most importantly, they will push the designer to think through a stimulating and expansive spectrum of possible scenarios.

Urban design today, especially in the global arena, has evolved new hybrid forms of practice that often result in richer versions of earlier conventional practices. As such, the practice has evolved to become more inclusive, recognizing its dependency on a multitude of actors and agencies for implementation and numerous fields for its design. As a practice, it has more fully embraced landscape, planning, and the integration of collaborators. Incremental strategies and multifaceted feedback loops are integral to this emerging approach and are causing the process of urban design to become increasingly dynamic. New technologies facilitate this in a more nuanced, finely grained, and grounded registrar of the reality we operate in. The process challenges conventional notions of urban design and dissipates the differences between developing tools for advocacy and engaging in advocacy—creating new models that combine both. Sometimes these are differentiated, but today, to be effective, they are often collapsed into a singular entity or process. Urban design is about how these spatial possibilities play out to influence our quality of life, economy, society, evolving culture, natural systems, resources, and the broader well-being of the planet. It is this extensive view of planetary implications and ecological thinking that will root questions of equity and humanism into our operations. Finally, the critical choice for us is between being a thermometer or a thermostat—to read the temperature or to change it. While we need both, in the end it is the instrumentality of designs that are socially and ecologically engaged and intellectually elastic that will be relevant for the future. This would necessarily have to be the touchstone for the next generation of designers who will be challenged by situating their practice in a landscape of flux—political, social, ecological, and most importantly demographic!

The journey through this book reasserts the notion that the urban designer is really a contemporary practicing polymath. One who directs dialogue-based processes—for imagining spatial possibilities means directing movement, lifestyle, morals, and the interaction of individuals. This makes urban design highly influential and the notion of the polymath becomes particularly important. We cannot avoid these conditions and disjuncture when forming the core agendas of our disciplines. Besides the question of scale—beyond regionalism to planetary urbanism and the broadening of the narrative—the critical challenge for us is the narrow circumscription of our site of operation versus understanding the site as being mediated by and embedded within a larger scale of economic, social, and political processes. So then the question becomes one of using the opportunity to have a broader social and progressive impact as urban designers beyond the site of our projects. Can engaging with designing temporal landscapes play a critical transitionary role in the process of flux that the planet is experiencing? Can we design for an urban space that accommodates flux and temporal value? Can urban designers challenge the assumption that permanence matters? Can we design with a divided mind where we see the simultaneous validity of different forms of the built environment and can oscillate between the notion of the temporary and permanent as well as the built and unbuilt? Can we resolve the seemingly wicked problem of accommodating a growing and shifting demography while touching the ground lightly and intervening minimally in our fragile ecosystem? This book guides us strategically to focus on these complex challenges and equips us to potentially instrumentalize urban design in the future.

The Urgency for a Radical Redesign of Our Urban Environment

Dutch urban design emerged in Delft as a response to the social issues arising from factory and industrial conditions in the Netherlands. People demanded more space, a better quality of life, improved hygiene, and attention to urban planning. This led to a period of urban expansion, marked by styles such as modern additions, garden villages, and post-war modernist developments. Urban planners, architects, landscape architects, and civil engineers all played a crucial role, working to meet the growing demand for housing, infrastructure, jobs, and amenities, shaping cities through large-scale land subdivision and traffic planning.

Today, cities face even greater challenges. Along with housing shortages, crises like climate change, water scarcity, air quality, and social segregation have converged in urban areas. But cities no longer have the luxury of endless expansion. To protect the surrounding landscape and ensure accessibility, cities must remain compact. This means that urban designers must now engage with the existing urban fabric to bring about transformation from within, assessing challenges at various scales and integrating solutions from multiple disciplines.

While urban design can operate at any scale, the microscale in established urban areas presents a key opportunity. Places with existing identity, where people are already engaged, offer fertile ground for urban transformation. These localized projects can expand to influence broader urban policies, improving city life as a whole.

This publication is the result of dialogue and reflection on urban design between practitioners and academia. It comes with one intention in mind: to provide students in urban design and associated disciplines—the future generation and eager designers—with inspiration and optimism about the possibility of designing better cities for all, in a radically inclusive way.

Each of our personal, educational, and professional trajectories has exposed us to different schools of urban design, bridging North and South America, India, Switzerland, and Spain with the Delft approach. With this book, we honor those traditions, while at the same time not aiming to be representative of any of them. This book is simply a personal interpretation, synthesis, and reflection on urban design that we believe poses relevant questions for the contemporary practice of urban design.

This is neither a theory or methods book nor a manual. We avoid discussing urban design in a dogmatic or normative way. In the past decades, urban design has evolved into a diverse set of complementary forms of practice. It would be absurd to claim that just one type of approach is central, and too bold of us to offer specific solutions. Urban design handbooks could end up doing more harm than good if they lead to universal solutions that do not account for the rich local social and ecological contexts.

Yet there is a lot to do in certain directions if we are to address the challenges we face, particularly growing social inequality and the climate emergency. To playfully emphasize that there is quite some homework to do, we chose the format of an exercise book. Using the concept of deep conviviality, we put forward a set of values that we believe should guide urban design projects in the twenty-first century, together with some supporting facts, theory, history, and imagination. You can call this a gentle manifesto, or a conversation starter about going beyond social and ecological inclusivity. In parallel, we provide 20 prompts for design exercises that we hope will make you think about design differently.

As in a studio class, we cannot tell you what your design should look like, but strive to provide you with a sense of direction. We have done our best to find the right balance between practicality and imagination. It must be you, the future urban designer, who finds the answers that best fit and bring about positive change in your own context.

This book is for those interested in designing radical changes to our living environment—an environment that resonates across global, regional, neighborhood, and individual scales, connecting humans and non-humans alike. We face multiple crises, and there is no time to waste; we must act swiftly to make a significant impact. Design challenges are evolving, and so must our approach. Change must come from within our cities, and from within the discipline of urban design. Most importantly, it must come from within us, the designers. We must embrace the fluid nature of our work and networks of collaborators. Our work is a lifelong learning process, and exercising is key if we want to remain relevant.

Urban Design Must Change Course

Permeable Permanence Matters

While human settlements cover no more than 3 percent of the planet's surface,[1] the present and future of cities are intertwined, in a substantial and wicked way, with the human-made causes and effects of climate change. Fantasies of gaining control over nature are futile. On the one hand, sea level rise, extreme weather events such as floods, droughts, and storms, and the spread of tropical diseases have significant impacts on cities' infrastructure and housing, as well as on the health and livelihoods of many. On the other hand, according to the Intergovernmental Panel on Climate Change (IPCC), cities are major contributors to climate change, accounting for a large percentage of greenhouse gas emissions (estimates suggest around 70 percent of global CO2 emissions) and energy consumption.[2] At the same time, the number of people living in urban areas is projected to increase from 55 to 68 percent of the world's population by 2050.[3] On top of all this, inequality and segregation are increasing, creating significant challenges for the future social sustainability of cities. Cities seem to no longer be places that offer opportunities for everyone.[4]

→ Fig. 01

However, the IPCC highlights the critical role of cities in achieving significant emissions reductions and promoting climate-resilient and socially and ecologically inclusive development. Compact urban development, new forms of collective housing, social infrastructure, and the enhancement of carbon uptake and storage through bio-based building materials, permeable surfaces, and urban green and blue infrastructures are put forward as key strategies for achieving sustainability goals. Nonetheless, there is a global disparity in financing, with more funds allocated to grey and physical infrastructure than to green and social infrastructure, and insufficient investment in marginalized and informal communities. It seems that urbanization is outpacing the capacity of cities to meet the growing need for affordable housing, efficient transportation, essential services, and employment. At best, incremental actions are set in motion as a response. For a majority of urban areas, the result is uncoordinated growth in the form of financial speculation, sprawl, or informal settlements. As a result, urban land consumption is expanding at a rate that outstrips population growth by as much as 50 percent, according to the World Bank,[5] feeding a building value chain that is responsible for 40 per cent of carbon emissions worldwide.[6]

→ Fig. 02

Since the 1980s, every decade has been hotter than the one before it. What is more, starting in 2014 and regardless of the global temperature dataset we look at, each year has been the warmest ever on record.[7] Many urban environments have proven unprepared to respond to warmer temperatures and heat waves, negatively impacting the health and well-being of their inhabitants, particularly older people.[8] The costs of inaction are troubling. Environmental issues are not only a matter of health but are related at a fundamental level to people's rights and citizenship. For example, direct exposure of citizens to polluted air in larger urban areas has greater consequences for chronic pulmonary diseases, and a lack of green space has been associated with hypertension and anxiety disorders.[9] Emergency responses can be troubling, too, deepening inequalities and stigmatizing vulnerable population groups. In countries like Spain, it is now forbidden to work outdoors during high-temperature conditions.[10] Across the world, cooling centers and climate shelters are emerging as architectural typologies conceived to offer relief from the heat to city residents who cannot afford air conditioning at home.

→ Fig. 03

As Greta Thunberg famously said, our house is on fire, and yet we keep expanding it with inflammable materials. How can urban design move forward? Is it about stopping new building, as suggested by Charlotte Malterre-Barthes' *Moratorium on New Construction?* Or, in a similar vein, is it about challenging the assumption that permanence matters, as proposed by Rahul Mehrotra?[11] Both provocations offer powerful concepts to productively question some of the core principles guiding urban design, adding to the repertoire of the discipline-related questions of temporality as well as built resource care and stewardship. However, "doing almost nothing" before the spatial and material aspects provoking climate injustice have been overcome might offer little to those, human and non-human, engaged in the politics of living. As Mehrotra points out, new models of urban design must necessarily emerge, but they should not be used as an argument to absolve the state from its responsibility to engage in planning and design for the common good. Urban design must ensure that the situated and specific struggles of all beings for decent living space, health, and infrastructure are recognized and addressed. Even more so because of the interdependencies between our own wellbeing and that of others—human and non-human—which we illustrate next.

Fig. 01 "Warming stripe" graph showing global change in temperature as measured over the past 100+ years. Source: Ed Hawkins, National Centre for Atmospheric Science, University of Reading.

Fig. 02 Unsustainable forms of urban land consumption are expanding at a rate that outstrips population growth. Photo: Jorge Taboada, *Escobedo, Nuevo León*, from the series "Alta Densidad" (2011) / Courtesy of Jorge Taboada.

Fig. 03 Climate inequalities are exemplified by the mainstreaming of cooling centers for urban populations who cannot afford air conditioning at home. Climate refuge at the Circulo de Bellas Artes in Madrid, Spain (2024). Photo: Miguel Balbuena / Courtesy of the Círculo de Bellas Artes.

Spatial Needs for Non-Human Companions

Cities are adopting nature-based solutions and green infrastructure to tackle many of the climate risks described above. Planting trees is a particularly popular solution, as trees are an accepted technology for carbon capture and health: they mitigate heat islands, promote active lifestyles, and reduce depression.[12] Powerful tree advocacy campaigns, like the 3-30-300 rule, are creating political awareness about the need to preserve and increase urban tree canopies.[13]

However, fulfilling the promise of tree planting does not come without challenges. For example, the way we design the cross-sections of streets and public spaces is crucial for the success of a planting campaign. Balancing the competing needs of people, plants, and animals in these confined areas is complicated. Impervious surfaces, limited space for roots, and underground infrastructural networks make it difficult for trees and other species to thrive. Despite these challenges, city infrastructure is still built with an emphasis on efficiency, prioritizing concrete and asphalt over greenspaces and water features. In the end, our urban design approach for the subsurface has not significantly changed since the grand projects of the nineteenth century—not to mention that trees are often deemed easily replaceable and fall victim to urban development.

→ Fig. 04 → Fig. 05 → Fig. 06

The implications of these issues are far-reaching and shape the prospects of a greener and more socially inclusive urban future. Time and space are crucial. For example, research tells us that carbon accumulation is higher at the later stages of a tree's lifetime[14] and that mature trees have a more positive impact on human health.[15] That is, urban trees need to be able to grow old and healthy to support our well-being. However, urban growth and transformation are causing a global decline in mature trees,[16] with cities losing millions of specimens to sealed surfaces.[17] Their removal is often justified by the replanting of new saplings. Yet hostile environmental and spatial conditions impact the health of new urban trees and those that remain. New trees "live fast, die young".[18] The small cubicles of soil we define as the living space for urban trees are too small. Trees are stressed and thirsty, undermining their cooling capacity.[19] Those that manage to survive are unhappy, impacting the wellbeing of human communities. This is often an unequal condition: research shows that wealthier neighborhoods tend to have more and healthier tree cover, while lower-income and minority communities often experience a lack of greenspace.[20] Overall, without truly accounting for the spatial needs of our non-human companions, we perpetuate exploitative notions of nature and entrenched social inequalities.

Nevertheless, we must be wary of the application of generic rules and solutions to these issues. In some contexts, it might simply be that there is little land available for tree planting. In the city of Mumbai, the total of all gardens and parks, playgrounds, recreation grounds, and encroached open spaces makes up about 5 percent of the total land of the city.[21] That equals roughly 1.1 square meters of open space per person. When compared to the 31 square meters of open space per capita in London—or the 26 in New York City, the struggles to reach some of the goals for greener, healthier, and more biodiverse cities across the many urban conditions worldwide become clear. It is not only a matter of species selection and soil quality but of high levels of coordination between city departments and difficult decisions to make space for other forms of urban life. The risk here is to prioritize ecological discourse as an elixir for what ails our cities, finding space at the expense of deepening uneven social dynamics caused by urbanization that result in instances of ecological gentrification or bourgeois environmentalism.[22]

At the core of the challenge depicted above is the need for a fundamental shift in the values that guide design practice as well as in the nature of the design process. Prioritizing ecological and social well-being—happy trees and happy people—over short-term efficiency demands a different way of thinking—one that embraces complexity rather than simplifying it. Forms of design practice that rely on linear, solution-oriented approaches, and compartmentalize the design process can limit the potential for transformation, and fail to account for these broader social and ecological challenges that cities face. As a result, design outcomes risk being superficial, ignoring the broader systemic implications. Changing our position as designers to embrace a renewed set of values guiding design with future interventions requires change from within the design process. Such a value-driven approach to design emphasizes a more fluid, iterative process—one that fosters critical reflection, collaboration, and integration across disciplines. The exercises in this book are designed to operationalize the shift in values reflected in the chapters that follow, encouraging you to engage deeply with social and ecological considerations through iterative, collaborative design processes that reflect the complexity of real-world challenges.

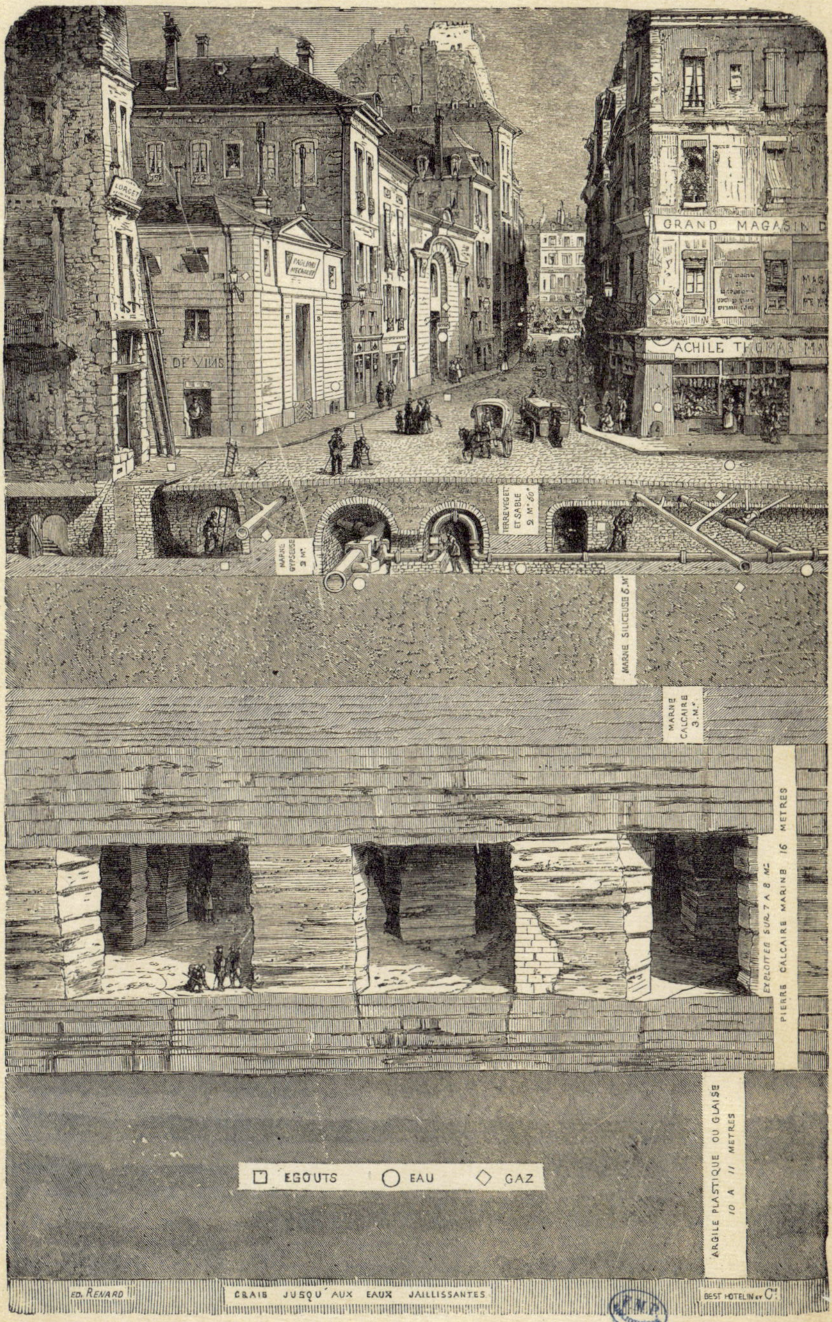

F. Roy, éditeur. — 300. Imp. Charaire et fils.

Le dessus et le dessous de Paris.

Fig. 04 The design of the urban subsurface has not changed much since the nineteenth century. Renard, *Le dessus et le dessous de Paris* (1852). Collection BIU Santé (Paris), ref. CISB0111.

Fig. 05 Painted markings on the pavement suggest an underground infrastructure of pipes and telecom cables. Photo: Ged Carroll / Creative Commons Attribution 2.0 Generic License.

Fig. 06 The complexity and density of underground infrastructure networks can be seen in this view of a street in Rotterdam, Netherlands from below. Source: Rotterdam 3D viewer / Gemeente Rotterdam.

1 Neil Brenner and Nikos Katsikis, "Operational Landscapes: Hinterlands of the Capitalocene", *Architectural Design 90*, no. 1 (January/February 2020): 22–31.

2 IPCC, *Climate Change 2022: Impacts, Adaptation, and Vulnerability: Contribution of Working Group II to the Sixth Assessment Report of the Intergovernmental Panel on Climate Change*, eds. Hans-Otto Pörtner et al. (Cambridge, UK: Cambridge University Press, 2022), https://doi.org/10.1017/9781009325844.

3 United Nations, Department of Economic and Social Affairs, Population Division, *World Urbanization Prospects: The 2018 Revision* (2018).

4 See: Maarten Van Ham, Tiit Tammaru, Rūta Ubarevičienė, and Heleen Janssen, eds., *Urban Socio-Economic Segregation and Income Inequality: A Global Perspective* (Cham, Switzerland: Springer Nature, 2021).

5 World Bank Group, "Urban Development", 2024, https://www.worldbank.org/en/topic/urbandevelopment/overview.

6 Gim Huay Neo and Yvonne Zhou, "The Building Sector Is Key to the Fight Against Climate Change", *World Economic Forum*, 26 June 2024, https://www.weforum.org/agenda/2024/06/building-sector-climate-change-construction-materials/.

7 United Nations, "WMO Confirms 2023 as Warmest Year on Record by a Huge Margin", 12 January 2024, https://news.un.org/en/story/2024/01/1145457.

8 See, for example, Frank van der Hoeven and Alex Wandl, *Hotterdam: How Space Is Making Rotterdam Warmer, How This Affects the Health of Its Inhabitants, and What Can Be Done About It* (Delft: TU Delft Open, 2018), https://repository.tudelft.nl/islandora/object/uuid:6abf1b9c-36ac-44d9-8fff-3ce2472a135c?collection=research.

9 Nathália Villa Dos Santos et al., "Accumulation of Trace Element Content in the Lungs of São Paulo City Residents and Its Correlation to Lifetime Exposure to Air Pollution", *Scientific Reports* 12, no. 1 (2022): 11083, https://doi.org/10.1038/s41598-022-15048-2; Tiana C. L. Moreira et al., "Assessing the Impact of Urban Environment and Green Infrastructure on Mental Health: Results from the São Paulo Megacity Mental Health Survey", *Journal of Exposure Science & Environmental Epidemiology* 32, no. 2 (2022): 205–12, https://doi.org/10.1038/s41370-021-00349-x.

10 *Real Decreto-ley 4/2023*, BOE núm. 113 (Madrid: 12 May 2023).

11 Rahul Mehrotra and Felipe Vera, eds., *Ephemeral Urbanism: Cities in Constant Flux* (Santiago, Chile: ARQ Ediciones, 2016); Charlotte Malterre-Barthes, "A Moratorium on New Construction? Beyond the Provocation: A Call for Systemic Change from Access to Housing to Construction Protocols", *Harvard Graduate School of Design*, 7 February 2023, https://www.gsd.harvard.edu/2023/02/a-moratorium-on-new-construction-beyond-the-provocation-a-call-for-systemic-change-from-access-to-housing-to-construction-protocols/.

12 Jared M. Ulmer et al., "Multiple Health Benefits of Urban Tree Canopy: The Mounting Evidence for a Green Prescription", *Health & Place* 42 (November 2016): 54–62, https://doi.org/10.1016/j.healthplace.2016.08.011; Roeland Samson et al., "Urban Trees and Their Relation to Air Pollution", in *The Urban Forest*, vol. 7 of *Future City*, eds. David Pearlmutter et al. (Cham: Springer, 2017), https://doi.org/10.1007/978-3-319-50280-9_3; Hiemstra, Saaroni, and Amorim, "The Urban Heat Island: Thermal Comfort and the Role of Urban Greening", in *The Urban Forest: Future City*, vol. 7, eds. David Pearlmutter et al. (Cham: Springer, 2017), https://doi.org/10.1007/978-3-319-50280-9_2; Gregory N. Bratman et al., "The Impacts of Nature Experience on Human Cognitive Function and Mental Health", *Annals of the New York Academy of Sciences* 1249 (February 2012): 118–36, https://doi.org/10.1111/j.1749-6632.2011.06400.x.

13 Cecil Konijnendijk, "The 3-30-300 Rule for Urban Forestry and Greener Cities", *Biophilic Cities Journal* 4, no. 2 (May 2022): 12–15.

14 Michael Köhl, Prem R. Neupane, and Neda Lotfiomran, "The Impact of Tree Age on Biomass Growth and Carbon Accumulation Capacity: A Retrospective Analysis Using Tree Ring Data of Three Tropical Tree Species Grown in Natural Forests of Suriname", *PLOS ONE* 12, no. 8 (August 2017): e0181187, https://doi.org/10.1371/journal.pone.0181187.

15 Dengkai Chi et al., "Residential Exposure to Urban Trees and Medication Sales for Mood Disorders and Cardiovascular Disease in Brussels, Belgium: An Ecological Study", *Environmental Health Perspectives* 130, no. 5 (May 2022): 57003, https://doi.org/10.1289/EHP9924.

16 David B. Lindenmayer, William F. Laurance, and Jerry F. Franklin, "Global Decline in Large Old Trees", Science 338, no. 6112 (December 2012): 1305–6, https://doi.org/10.1126/science.1231070.

17 David J. Nowak and Eric J. Greenfield, "Declining Urban and

Community Tree Cover in the United States", *Urban Forestry & Urban Greening* (May 2018), https://doi.org/10.1016/j.ufug.2018.03.006.

18 Ian A. Smith, Victoria K. Dearborn, and Lucy R. Hutyra, "Live Fast, Die Young: Accelerated Growth, Mortality, and Turnover in Street Trees", *PLOS ONE* 14, no. 5 (May 2019): e0215846, https://doi.org/10.1371/journal.pone.0215846.

19 Aleksandar Rankovic, "A Stroll through the Critical Zone: Exploring the Agency of Trees, Soils, and Microbes in the Streets of Paris", in *Critical Zones: The Science and Politics of Landing on Earth*, eds. Bruno Latour and Peter Weibel (Cambridge, MA: MIT Press, 2020), 150-153; Ambre David, Anaïs Boura, Aleksandar Rankovic, Jérôme Ngao, and others, "Long Term Impact of Climate on Tree-Growth Patterns in Paris Street Trees and Its Consequences on Tree Cooling Potential: A Dendroclimatic Approach", presented at the 9th International Conference on Urban Climate and 12th Symposium on the Urban Environment, Toulouse, June 2015, https://www.researchgate.net/publication/281235706_Long_term_impact_of_climate_on_tree-growth_patterns_in_Paris_street_trees_and_its_consequences_on_tree_cooling_potential_A_dendroclimatic_approach.

20 For cities like Boston, increasing tree canopy in low-income neighborhoods is seen as a strategy for equity and inclusion of all citizens. *Urban Forest Plan* (City of Boston, September 2022), https://www.boston.gov/sites/default/files/file/2022/09/urban_forest_plan_final_092022.pdf. Also see: Dexter Locke, Billy Hall, J. M. Grove, Steward T. Pickett, Laura A. Ogden, Carissa Aoki, Christopher G. Boone, et al., "Residential Housing Segregation and Urban Tree Canopy in 37 US Cities," *SocArXiv*, 6 January 2020, https://doi.org/10.1038/s42949-021-00022-0.

21 "Open Mumbai: An Exhibition on How We Can Expand Public Spaces", National Gallery of Modern Art, Mumbai, 16 March 2012 to 7 April 2012, https://ngmaindia.gov.in/pdf/open-mumbai-pic1.pdf.

22 Amita Baviskar, "Between Violence and Desire: Space, Power, and Identity in the Making of Metropolitan Delhi", *International Social Science Journal* 55, no. 175 (March 2003): 89–98, https://doi.org/10.1111/1468-2451.5501009; Raquel Hädrich Silva, Margreet Zwarteveen, Dominic Stead, and Taneha Kuzniecow Bacchin, "Bringing Ecological Urbanism and Urban Political Ecology to Transformative Visions of Water Sensitivity in Cities", Cities 145 (February 2024), https://doi.org/10.1016/j.cities.2023.104685.

Inverse and Reverse

As a designer, you can take a leap into the future by, for example, turning the strategy for a potential problem 180 degrees and fully leveraging it as an unstoppable engine for solving problems on various scales.

In doing so, try to keep the idea as extreme as possible and reverse the practical problems you encounter along the way into solutions that rise from opposite thinking. This might result in an exercise that provides an inspiring and unexpected answer to a posed problem.

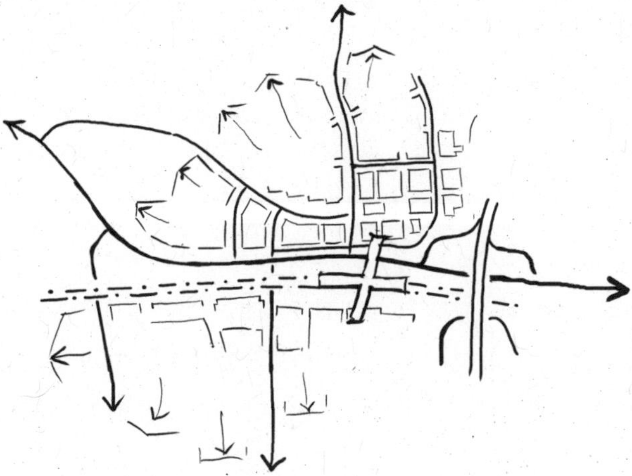

TRADITIONAL CITY EXPANSION
ALONG INFRASTRUCTURE AND RIGID
BUILDING BLOCKS.

LANDSCAPE INTERVENTIONS
AS A CARRYING FRAMEWORK FOR
SOCIAL ECOLOGICAL CITY DEVELOPMENT

What If ... to the Max!

During the design process and the further development of interesting options, one inevitably comes across impossibilities and obstacles that, due to practical habituation, carry an ingrained solution that potentially weakens the concept. When you recognize a blockage, it can be interesting to immediately ask the question "what if" and then intuitively outline a few options that entail extreme solutions to the posed problem. Closed becomes open, inaccessible becomes accessible, use becomes reuse, and a barrier becomes a connection.

Pushing these thoughts to the extreme increases the chance of success, since it takes a lot to visualize a potential problem as a layered opportunity. To do this, it must be made clear that by tackling a stated problem, multiple opportunities arise for the project, on multiple layers. And the sum of the parts is therefore higher than the possible extra investment involved.

WHAT IF?

NO SPACE FOR DEEP SOIL IN THE DENSIFYING CITY?

ARCHITECTURE IS THE CARRIER OF DEEP SOIL CONDITIONS...

PARKING LEADS TO AN UNATTRACTIVE BLOCKED CITY?

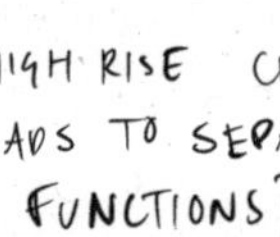

... MOBILITY BECOMES AN ATTRACTIVE PART AS A CONNECTED CITY IN THE CITY...

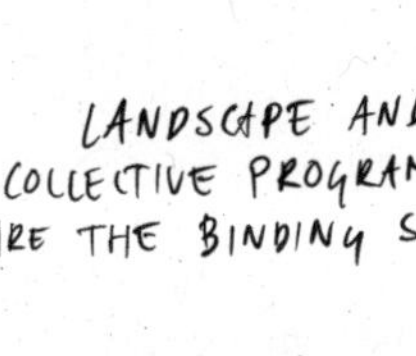

HIGH RISE CITY LEADS TO SEPARATED FUNCTIONS?

LANDSCAPE AND COLLECTIVE PROGRAM ARE THE BINDING SPINE...

Intersect and Reflect

Repeatedly cutting through a design project makes the spatial possibilities richer. The urban designer should not stop at the façade but should cut across several dimensions. Think through the buildings, involve the sky and the ground, and stop sketching when you feel that relevance is waning.

This creates an urban design cross-section that, in addition to spatial principles, also includes social experience, sustainable systems, rootscapes on different levels, and ideas for programming. It is important to make these intersections in multiple phases and always reflect on them from the higher scale level using area cross sections and maps.

Consider making these reflections thematic instead of integral, so that the different themes become recognizable and you reduce the complexity of your design project to a clear and understandable level.

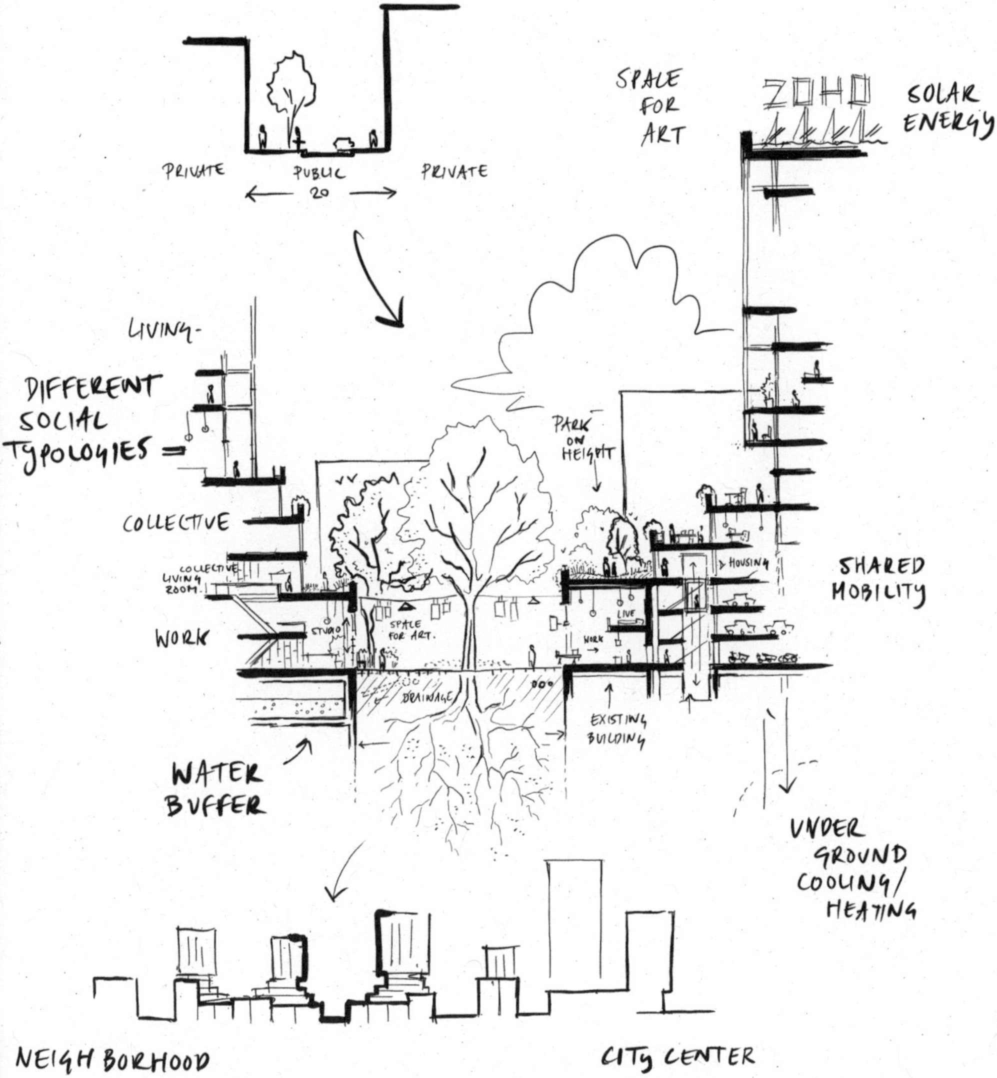
PRIVATE
PUBLIC
20
PRIVATE
SPACE FOR ART
ZOHO
SOLAR ENERGY
LIVING-
DIFFERENT SOCIAL TYPOLOGIES =
COLLECTIVE
COLLECTIVE LIVING ROOM
WORK
STUDIO
SPACE FOR ART.
PARK ON HEIGHT
HOUSING
LIVE
WORK
SHARED MOBILITY
DRAINAGE
EXISTING BUILDING
WATER BUFFER
UNDER GROUND COOLING/ HEATING
NEIGHBORHOOD
CITY CENTER

Technical Deep Dive

When open space is limited in a city, the role of design art within engineering becomes increasingly important. Researching and implementing the latest innovations in a new urban system is essential. Understand that you cannot know everything. It is valuable to engage with (technical) experts, innovators, and related disciplines to test and refine your initial ideas concerning climate, nature, and social cohesion.

Continue writing, drawing, and discussing with each other. Challenge the experts, but also critically assess their proposals. From a perspective of total integration, we encounter limitations, meaning that compromises will need to be made. By examining the functionality, feasibility, and buildability of various components, they can be reflected upon within the context of the overall sustainable urban system. Maintain this feedback loop throughout the design process.

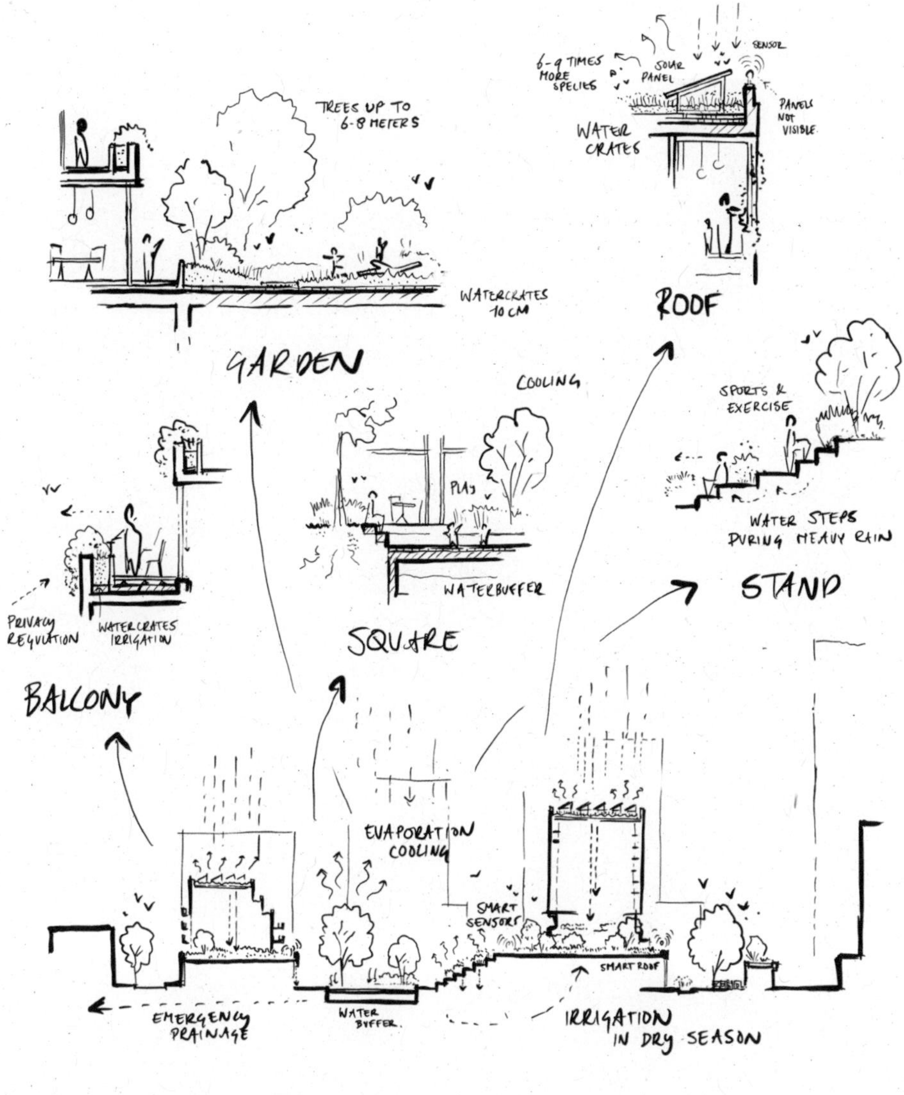

BIOCLIMATE ENGINEERING

Urban Design for Social and Ecological Interplay

Understanding Flexibility, Adaptation, and Reciprocity

Have you ever wondered what your city looked like before it was a city? It is always a fascinating exercise to go far back in time, discover its original ecology, and compare it to what we have today. Depending on the geography, geology, and climate, we might find natural landscapes that were highly dynamic and constantly changing. Fresh and salt water, sand deposits, clay, peat, and loam soil, and the alternation between rocky and soft surfaces may have provided fertile land. Gradients, variations, and interactions provided all kinds of possible feeding and breeding grounds. It was a living ecosystem with high dynamics—one that could flow without boundaries, where various plant, animal, and human species were able to grow, flourish, and develop.

→ Fig. 07

In various places in the world, at different times, human inventions have made it possible to cultivate the land and to combine hunting and gathering with a more permanent existence in small settlements. For example, in the Netherlands, combined residential farmhouses were built from locally found, dug, or grown building materials such as reeds, loam, clay, willow branches, and oak supporting structures (today, we call these biomaterials). Archaeological evidence and reconstructions show that these architectures had an open character.[1] Façades were used to dry laundry, dry and salt meat, and to bake and dry pots together with others from the community. The organic disposition of buildings, which was related to optimal sunlight collection and the direction of the wind, harnessing the breeze for cooling, formed a collective and multifunctional yard and joint open structure. Those who lived there established an environment based on different social domains:

an interplay and composition of collective, private, social, and semi-public spaces.
→ Fig. 08

Settlements began to develop along existing landscape structures, often higher ridges in the typically Dutch wet and marshy areas, as well as along waterways. These natural ridges were crucial to the early growth of urban areas. For instance, The Hague was established along coastal dunes, and the city's layout still reflects the importance of these natural features. In addition to hunting and gathering, people in the immediate vicinity grew various vegetables, legumes, nuts, and seeds. The ridges provided ideal routes for people and goods to travel along.

These first communities can be seen as a two-hour environment. People might have had a radius of 15 kilometers around the community within which they lived self-sufficiently, in balance with nature, the climate, and their fellow human beings. The dangers of nature and changing weather were recognized and integrated, leading to an adaptive and flexible lifestyle. By keeping the buildings and structures demountable, people in the early settlements were flexible and accustomed to the regular occurrence of natural disasters. Freshwater floods from the river were even welcomed, as they provided more fertile soil for the coming years. The communities built freshwater reservoirs and food storage that enabled them to survive such natural disasters. A flood from the sea would cause the community to pack up and settle on another, as safe as possible, river deposit. At that time, one could say that the ecological footprint was zero or in balance.

However, this grounded existence was also possible because only 3,000 people lived in what today is Dutch territory. As settlements grew, nature became a force to be controlled. In the Netherlands, this happened mostly through the construction of dikes during the eleventh and twelfth centuries, a period that saw the growth of cities and expansion of polders and land due to receding water. As Marina Otero argues, the Dutch landscape became a designed landscape and a paradigmatic example of Cartesianism.[2] Descartes' imperative of rationalization and the separation of humans from nature (placing humanity in a superior position) had a vast influence, driving the subsequent industrial revolutions, capitalist models of urbanization, and domination of landscapes, resources, and others at the expense of ecological and ethical concerns. Most of our cities are still built with this mindset, and we encounter ourselves as the man in a notorious cartoon by Saul Steinberg, looking into nature while trapped in a Cartesian cube.

→ Fig. 09

Among this pervasive, darker side of modernity,[3] we still find examples that resist and manifest what we could call ecological and social conviviality. In the north of Iran, the traditional building form and its spatial organization and materiality are utterly dependent on climatic conditions. Houses are built on platforms to protect inhabitants from seasonal floods in a way that allows for growth and change over time, forming settlements that herald a spirit of openness between fellow residents and the landscape. In Chile's Atacama region, vernacular housing seeks equilibrium with the soil—an entity which is alive—and water resources, grounded in relationality and interdependency.

→ Fig. 10

Overall, people in different places and at various times have found the proper interaction, balance, and empowerment from the interplay of climate (nature), community (people), and building (technology). It is high time to bring alternative ways of thinking to the fore, which are largely missing from the development of major forms of practice. Direct appropriation of more-than-human or indigenous knowledge, however, will not work. We need to unlearn and then re-learn to appreciate, conserve, and re-invigorate the natural and cultural heritage of our living environment, of our context.

Today, the climate and environmental crisis is both an immediate consequence of modernization and an urgent call to develop a radical alternative. These changing conditions have been playing a pivotal role in calling for more holistic visions and designs for future types of urban environments. Addressing this crisis started in the early 1970s, but the warnings of the International Panel on Climate Change (IPCC) reports on climate change, starting in the 1990s, brought public and political awareness that resulted in programs for climate mitigation (e.g., energy transition, circular economy, clean technology) and adaptation (e.g., flood risk reduction, urban heat stress reduction). With national policies reclaiming space for nature, biodiversity, and green-blue networks,[4] it is critical to rethink how landscape intermingles in productive ways with urban development and supports the environmentalization of the city and its new economies.

Fig. 07 The salt marshes in Krabbenkreek, Zeeland (the Netherlands) are a highly dynamic ecosystem that provides a gradient of conditions for multispecies flourishing. Photo: Siebe Swart.

Fig. 08 Inspirational precedents of contemporary notions as biomaterial construction, bioclimatic design, and open architecture can be read as ancient ways of building and living, as exemplified in this reconstructed Iron Age farm in Dongen (the Netherlands). Photo: Toine Snoeren, Ijzertijdboerderij Dongen.

Fig. 09 The Cartesian imperative of rationalization and separation of humans from nature still dominates the general mindset shaping contemporary urban development. Saul Steinberg (1960), illustration included in *The Labyrinth.* © The Saul Steinberg Foundation, c/o Pictoright Amsterdam 2024.

Fig. 10 Knowledge present in vernacular architecture speaks about ways of building and living that are attuned to climate and landscape conditions. A two-story house with a pointed roof in the Safidrud delta, on display at the Gilan Rural Heritage Museum Rasht county, Gilan Province, Iran. Photo: MasoudK / Creative Commons Attribution Generic-Share Alike 3.0 Unported.

Encompassing Bodies and Ecosystems

Gilles Clément's critique of traditional urban landscaping practices highlights their exclusion of animals (human and non-human) and any plants beyond the gardener's control. This attitude mirrors the rigid and insular practices of the scientific community, which often operates in ways that feel disconnected from everyday life. Trees, in his view, have been reduced to mere technologies and ornaments of a bourgeois aesthetic.[5] Similarly, Emanuele Coccia urges us to reconsider our relationship with trees, viewing them not merely as passive green spots or data points in our environment but as dynamic guardians that condition our experience of the world.[6] As argued by Arturo Escobar, to achieve true health, we must address the entire system of relationships, encompassing both bodies and ecosystems. Healing, he insists, must occur within the context of place and community, challenging the conventional narratives of sustainable development.[7] Returning to trees, and by extension to a deeper relationship with other beings, does not imply a rejection of urban life but rather an opportunity to transform our cities from within. These perspectives urge us to see non-humans as living subjects integral to our own lives, embodying life and fostering a deeper connection between the urban and the natural.

Deep conviviality in urban design expresses the idea of radically living together with differences, of the possibility of humans and non-humans flourishing together in the city. We call it *deep* in reference to the concept of deep ecology, which advocates for a shift to ecocentrism and asserts the well-being and importance of all beings.[8] With the flourishing of all the other beings inextricably bound to our own existence, drawing from the work of Iván Illich, Allain Caillé, and others, we define conviviality as a way of living together (*con-vivere*) that allows humans to care for each other and for Nature, without denying the legitimacy of conflict, but moving forward to use it as a dynamizing and creativity-sparking force.[9] Conflict, an inherent condition of urban spaces, is a key factor. Achieving deep conviviality implies not just reformulating public space but also addressing issues of housing, mobility, and work. Metaphorical notions bridging different concepts, including urban ecology, urban nature, urban forest, ecological urbanism, and the biotope city, must deal imaginatively and in a more nuanced way with the situated, material, and organizational complexities and conflicts of the urban condition at the local scale to achieve just social and ecological coexistence.

In this context, urban design, a discipline concerned at its core with defining the boundaries between public and private, the program and utilization of space, and building guidelines and the design of public space,[10] appears as a powerful ally to other disciplines in adapting our cities to new climatic conditions. Not only that, but as a discipline that, as Mehrotra suggests, is "about design synthesis [...] and dissolving and resolving contestations through spatial arrangements," urban design can help us transcend unproductive binaries.[11] Serving as a bridge between the physical characteristics of a city, socio-economic demands, and government guidelines and regulations,[12] urban design seems suited to lead the integration of climate action in cities in a way that is both context-specific and fosters deep conviviality between the social, the built environment, and the ecological.

Designing for deep social and ecological conviviality may seem straightforward, but it's far from obvious—especially for those at the start of their careers and even for seasoned practitioners. The first step is recognizing that collaboration and integrating multidisciplinary knowledge are essential to creating socially and ecologically impactful designs. Urban design, planning, and landscape architecture are closely related but also demand insights from other fields—this is foundational to the Delft approach. Another key aspect is process, which emphasizes continuous iteration through analysis, design, and presentation.[13]

Analysis involves understanding complex conditions. Design leverages imagination and synthesis to creatively engage with this knowledge. Presentation is the moment to test ideas, communicate with the public, and foster collaboration. These three elements—analysis, design, and presentation—should be non-hierarchical, fast, and flexible, continuously alternating between exploration and interpretation. This dynamic process leads to insights that fuel the next design step. However, not every path leads to a breakthrough—some may stop at a dead end.

We developed the exercises in this book to help you cultivate a personalized design workflow that makes you more aware of your work methods and of what fosters your growth. The proposed sequence follows an iterative flow of converging and diverging moments. In each phase of opening and closing, these exercises sharpen your ideas, structuring the process towards a final design. Even as the design settles, new workflows may emerge, bringing fresh insights and creativity. The design process resembles a river—meandering and branching—where moments of exploration and self-awareness are crucial for achieving an integrated socio-ecological design.

Similar to many urban designers, landscape architects, architects, educators, activists, and other professionals, we advocate for a dramatic turnaround in our approach to design and a call for radical thinking and imagination. Infrastructure, economy, and buildings should no longer be central. Ecological and social matters must simultaneously be at the forefront of the design process. Certainly, we must make designs that are economically viable, actionable, and attainable, but ecological and social values must come first, meaning we must design and work together differently. Interdisciplinary approaches become paramount for building sufficient understanding and expertise in the social, ecological, and urban domains. Before starting, we should also understand where we came from and use a historical and theoretical lens to see where we stand in our task of rebuilding urban ecologies of conviviality.

1 Harry Fokkens, "The Longhouse as a Central Element in Bronze Age Daily Life", in *Bronze Age and Iron Age Communities in North-Western Europe*, eds. Jean Bourgeois, Ignace Bourgeois, and Bart Cherretté (Brussels: Vlaams Kennis- en Cultuurforum, 2003), 9–38; Stijn Arnoldussen and Harry Fokkens, eds., *Bronze Age Settlements in the Low Countries* (Oxford: Oxbow Books, 2008), https://doi.org/10.2307/j.ctt1cfr8w0.

2 Marina Otero Verzier, "Cartesian Enclosures", in *New Geographies* 12, The Commons, eds. Mojdeh Mahdavi and Lian Wang (April 2022): 39–57.

3 Walter D. Mignolo, *The Darker Side of Western Modernity: Global Futures, Decolonial Options* (Durham, NC: Duke University Press, 2011).

4 Notably, the Biodiversity Strategy of the European Green Deal: European Commission, *Communication from the Commission to the European Parliament, the Council, the European Economic and Social Committee and the Committee of the Regions: EU Biodiversity Strategy for 2030. Bringing Nature Back into Our Lives* (European Commission, 2020), https://eur-lex.europa.eu/legal-content/EN/TXT/?uri=CELEX:52020DC0380.

5 Gilles Clément, "*The Planetary Garden" and Other Writings.* Philadelphia: University of Pennsylvania Press, 2015.

6 Emanuelle Coccia, "Experiencing the World", in *Trees*, eds. Bruce Albert, Francis Halle, and Stefano Mancuso (Paris: Fondation Cartier pour l'art contemporain, 2019), 24–31.

7 Arturo Escobar, "Healing the Web of Life: On the Meaning of Environmental and Health Equity", *International Journal of Public Health* 64, no. 3–4 (January 2019), https://doi.org/10.1007/s00038-018-1154-y.

8 Arne Naess, "The Shallow and the Deep, Long-Range Ecology Movement: A Summary", Inquiry 16, no. 1–4 (January 1973): 95–100, https://doi.org/10.1080/00201747308601682.

9 Inspired by *Convivialist Manifesto: A Declaration of Interdependence (Global Dialogues 3)* (Duisburg: Käte Hamburger Kolleg / Centre for Global Cooperation Research (KHK / GCR21), 2014), https://doi.org/10.14282/2198-0403-GD-3.

10 Meyer, Hoekstra, and Westrik, *Urbanism: Fundamentals and Prospects* (Amsterdam: Boom Uitgevers, 2020).

11 Rahul Mehrotra, "The Permanent and the Ephemeral: What Does This Mean for Urbanism", in *The Kinetic City & Other Essays* (Berlin: Architangle, 2021), 268.

12 Rahul Mehrotra, "Imaginations Beyond Architecture", in *The Informal Economy Revisited: Examining the Past, Envisioning the Future*, eds. Martha Chen and Françoise Carré (London: Routledge, 2020), 132–35.

13 Explained in a position document by Rients Dijkstra, Maarten van Ham, Steffen Nijhuis, and Machiel van Dorst, along with the input of many others, the Delft Approach refers to a unique way of thinking and doing urbanism. Built on a long legacy of integration of urban and landscape design, with planning and engineering, this approach aspires to better satisfy human needs, and to achieve fairer, healthier, and more resilient urban landscapes. Our reflection and proposition on a more fluid design process is largely inspired by this approach. Specifically, the deep collaboration of Víctor Muñoz Sanz with Rients Dijkstra and the several generations of students that went through the intensive course "Elements of the Delft Approach" underpins a lot of the thinking behind this book. This course was designed to support master students in gaining critical awareness on their design process, through the iterative integration of research and analysis with design and presentation.

Dig Into Hidden History

It is interesting to continue writing and drawing during your historical research and analysis, using analytical diagrams and schemes to imagine how people lived together and how their living environment was organized. Can you distill your insights into a few core values or guiding themes that could be relevant in the further development of your design process?

FLEXIBLE COMMUNAL SPACE

FLEXIBLE FACADE

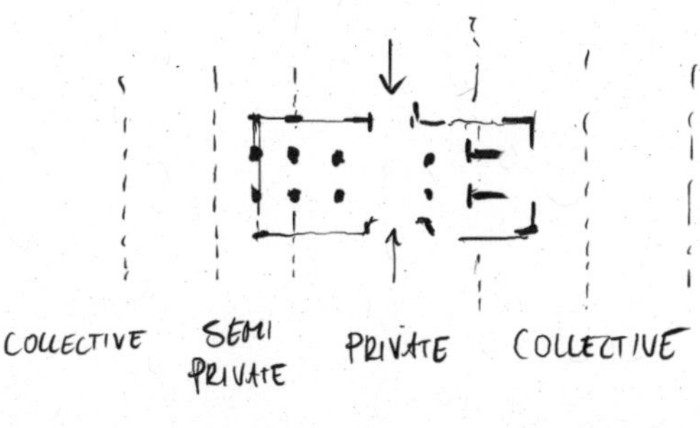

Unbounded Wandering

A self-sufficient society that is locally oriented and does not travel over long distances may seem like a utopia from bygone times. However, it can be interesting to undertake the analytical exercise of walking 20 minutes in every possible direction from an urban project area to explore the urban, ecological, and socio-cultural values and opportunities.

This approach can create an organically shaped, spider-like map that can be summarized using a clear vision diagram. What can your project add to foster new ecological connections and strengthen sustainable systems within this scope? What programs can you introduce so that people from different neighborhoods can meet, be encouraged to take initiative, and further develop their skills and interests?

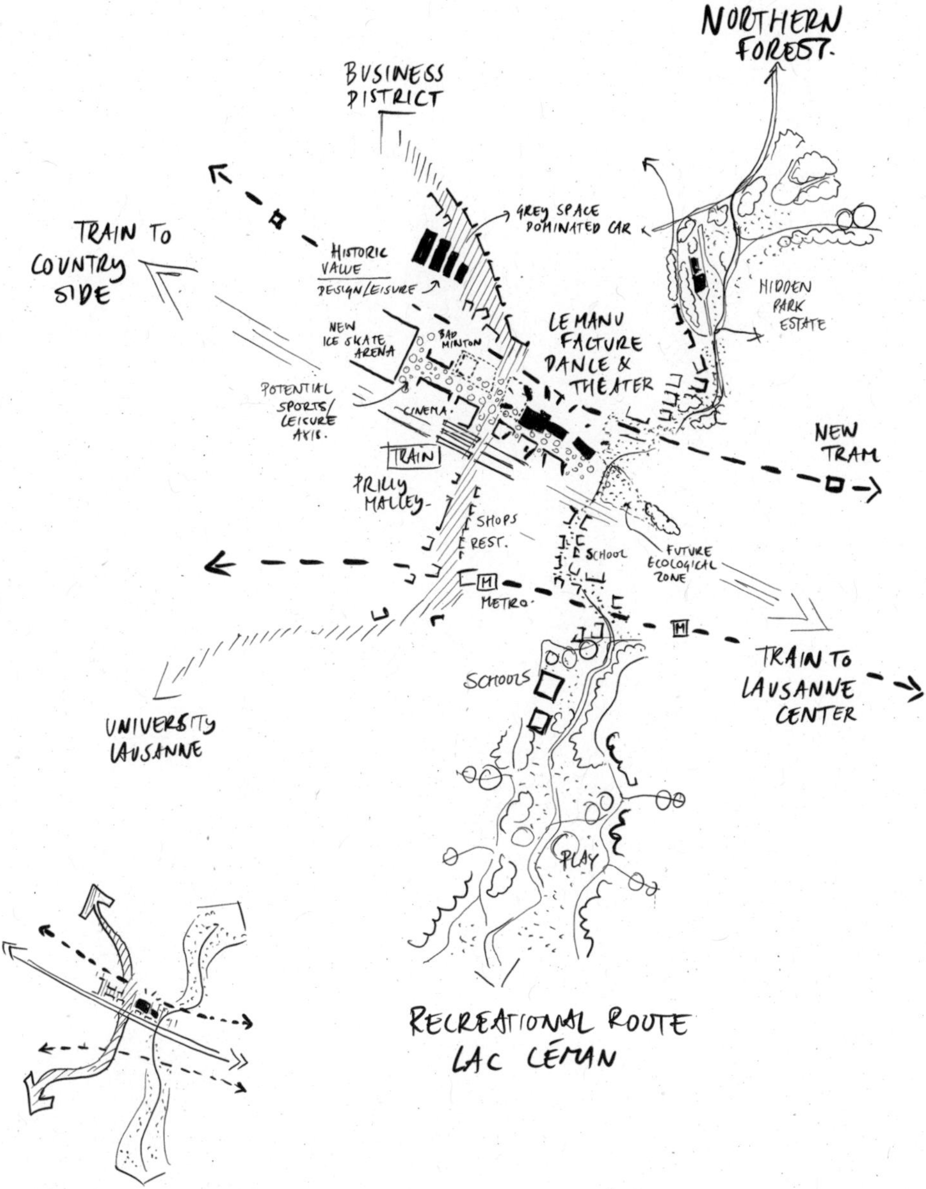
NORTHERN FOREST.
BUSINESS DISTRICT
GREY SPACE DOMINATED CAR
TRAIN TO COUNTRY SIDE
HISTORIC VALUE
DESIGN/LEISURE
HIDDEN PARK ESTATE
NEW ICE SKATE ARENA
BAD MINTON
LE MANU FACTURE DANCE & THEATER
POTENTIAL SPORTS/ LEISURE AXIS.
CINEMA.
TRAIN
NEW TRAM
PRILLY MALLEY.
SHOPS
REST.
SCHOOL
FUTURE ECOLOGICAL ZONE
METRO.
M
M
TRAIN TO LAUSANNE CENTER
SCHOOLS
UNIVERSITY LAUSANNE
PLAY
RECREATIONAL ROUTE LAC LÉMAN

Intercultural Inspiration

Stay curious about references and examples that align with your fascination and guiding theme throughout your design process. By seeking examples from different cultures, climates, and topographies, you can gain even more breadth of solutions offered and deeper insight into the sustainable and balanced interplay between people, nature, and the built environment.

Can these insights help you distill abstract values that you want to incorporate into your project? Can you identify how intelligent urban planning and architectural principles have made it possible for these sustainable examples to withstand the test of time? Which aspects cannot be applied to the context of your project, and why not?

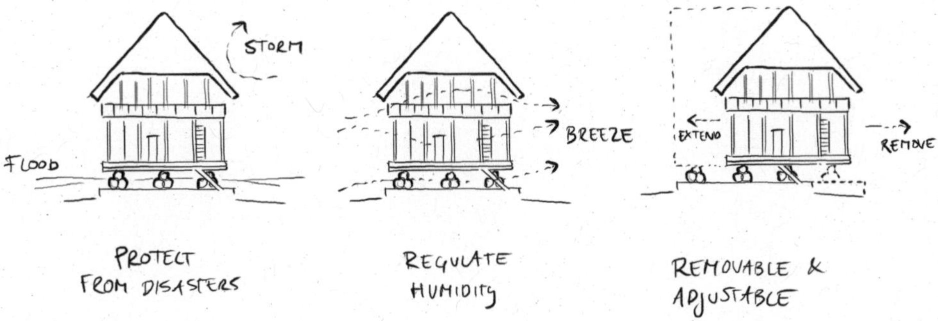
STORM
FLOOD
PROTECT FROM DISASTERS
BREEZE
REGULATE HUMIDITY
EXTEND
REMOVE
REMOVABLE & ADJUSTABLE

Verify and Validate

Investigating and analyzing recently realized projects helps you test and verify your ideas in contemporary practice. It also provides more insight into feasibility within today's technological and political contexts. This can vary by location and culture, so keep a broad perspective.

A reference can be stimulating as a whole project, but your design will become more inspiring, layered, and profound if you can understand and use the successes of various specific aspects in your own unique urban design project.

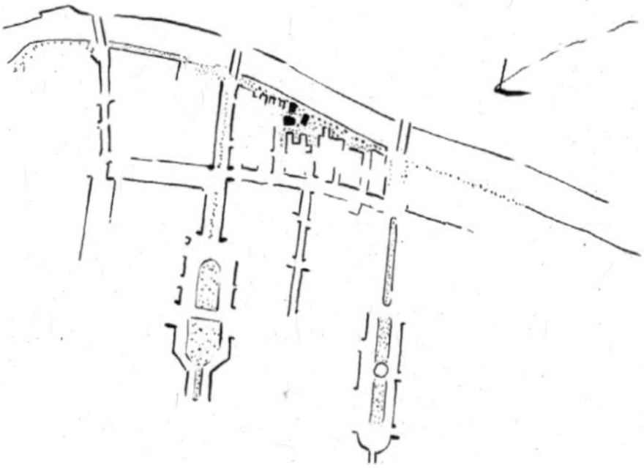

NESTLED BETWEEN RIVERBANK AND INDUSTRIAL URBAN STRUCTURES

OPEN PLINTHS WITH COLLECTIVE PROGRAM ACTIVATES COMMUNAL LANDSCAPE

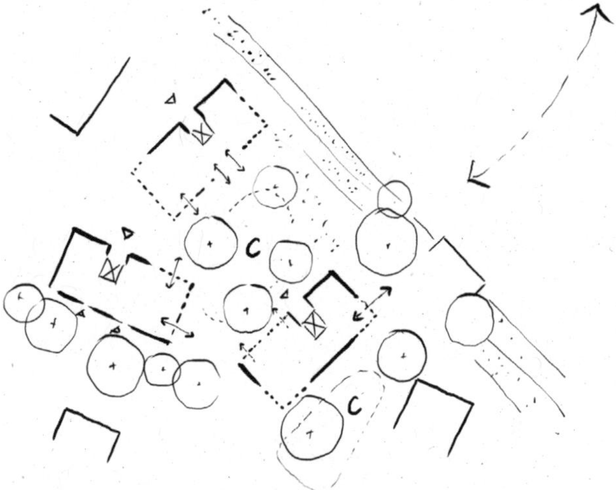

TILTED URBAN DESIGN CREATES SHELTERED SPACES AND LEAVES ROOM FOR EXISTING TREES

Unravel Ecosystems

To provide overview and insight, it can help to structure the research and design in natural, technical, and social ecosystems. This layered approach ensures an overview of related themes and way they influence each other.

The trick is to be able to analyze and design this layered approach separately while at the same time seeing and reflecting on the whole as an integral and powerful strategy. This iteration in layers provides clarity in the process and can also be very useful for non-professionals to maintain an overview and gain understanding of the project.

NATURAL

ECOSYSTEM

WATER
BIODIVERSITY
CLIMATE
PLANTATION
CULTURE HISTORY
SOIL
...

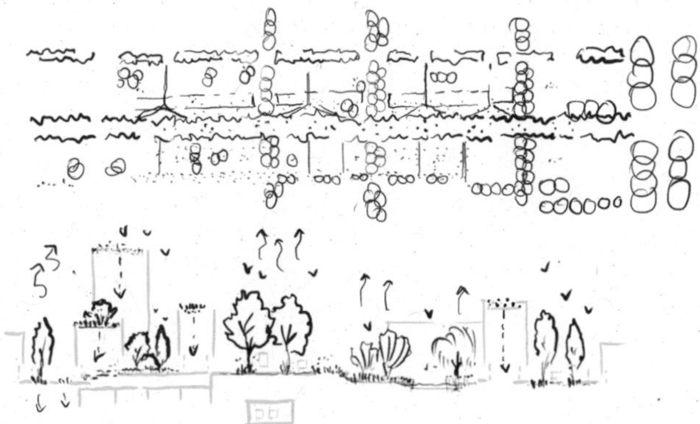

TECHNICAL

ECOSYSTEM

MOBILITY
MORPHOLOGY
SUSTAINABILITY
INFRASTRUCTURE
IT NETWORKS
BUILDINGS
....

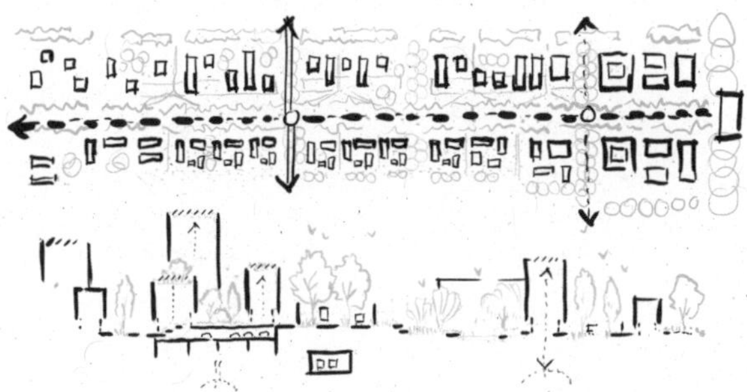

SOCIAL

ECOSYSTEM

PROGRAM
RECREATION
EDUCATION
COMMUNITIES
EXPERIMENT
PLAY & SPORT
....

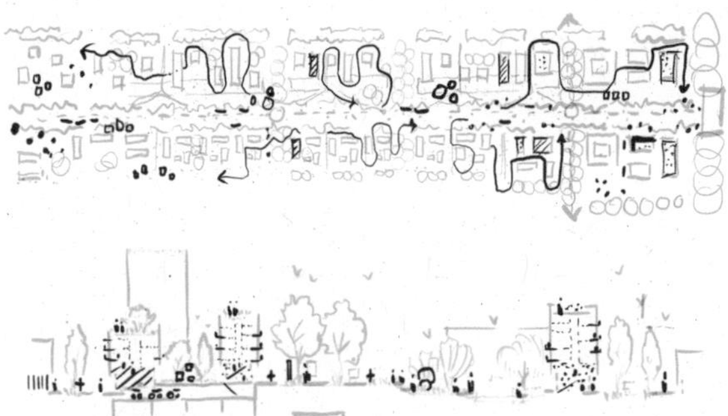

Evolutionary Tree

Be fast and agile. By quickly putting down solid ideas, you create an idea lab that you can draw as an evolutionary tree. This can help express your ideas clearly, forcing yourself to name them distinctively and precisely. Over and over again. By maintaining speed in the process and daring to make quick judgements based on your value compass, a continuous workflow emerges from which branches can arise that lead to nothing, or that grow together into new and unexpectedly flourishing integrations.

You can execute this workflow by yourself or with a group of designers. You can even consider undertaking such workshops with your clients and stakeholders, as the process shows your value as a designer and creates support and discussion about the most optimal solution within a short span of time.

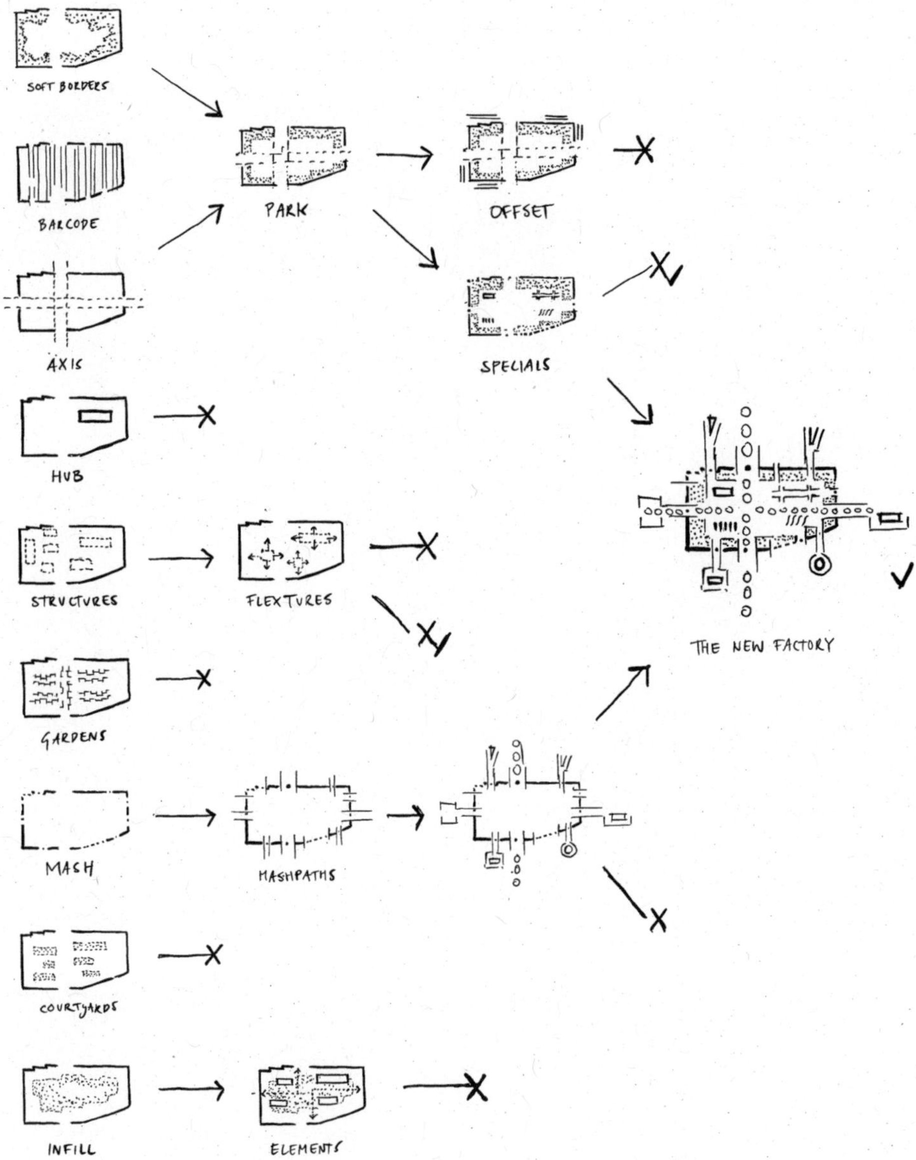
SOFT BORDERS
BARCODE
AXIS
HUB
STRUCTURES
GARDENS
MASH
COURTYARDS
INFILL
PARK
FLEXTURES
MASHPATHS
ELEMENTS
OFFSET
SPECIALS
THE NEW FACTORY

From Don't Know to Workflow

The creative design process is often depicted as an exploratory (chaotic or not) line, a line driven by the issues of the day that can go in all directions, but slowly converges towards the final design and presentation. Finding a way out of the confusion is seen as the result of a revelation, innate talent, or of tacit knowledge from years of experience in the field. All of these things matter, of course, but like others in related design and creative disciplines, we believe the process does not necessarily have to be a black box.

To enable a good conversation with one another, it can be interesting to draw this diagram in different ways or to give it more structure. A sequence of converging and diverging moments forms an ongoing iterative (feedback) loop. In the process, exercises and various methods help focus and sharpen design ideas, structuring the path to a final design.

In the further elaboration phase, it is likely that new workflows will branch out from the initial workflow. The design has settled somewhat, but is still being worked out. New design processes emerge at various points, which in turn require insight, inspiration, and variations. Keep your workflow open and recognize the moments when you are working on a (new) design assignment; it can help to (re)apply the right design methodologies at the right moment.

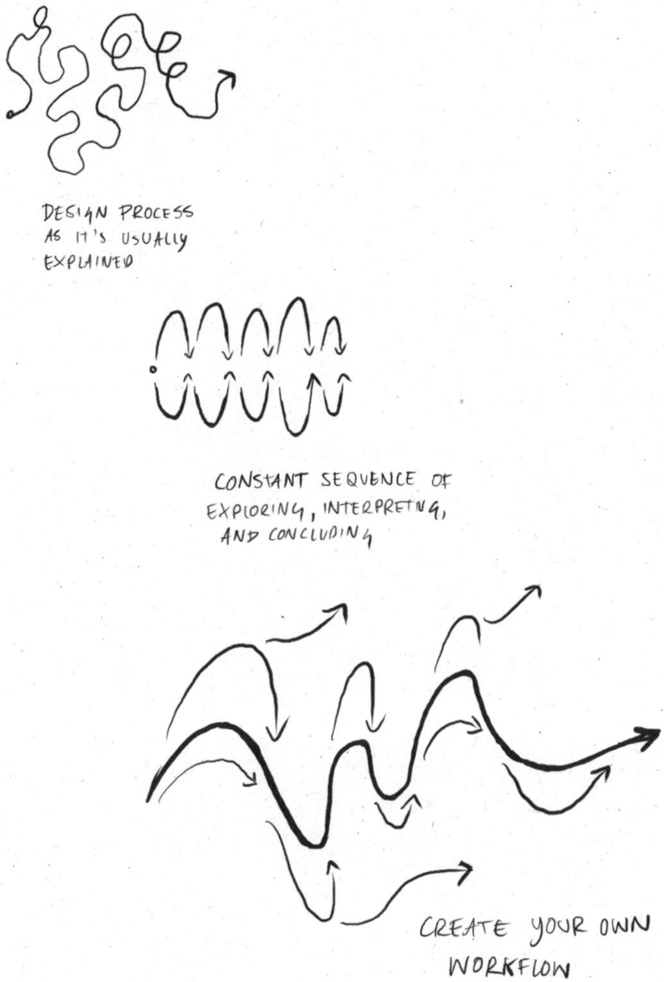

Urban Design Remains an Unfinished Composition

Rhythms of Straight Lines and Colors

In 1925, Dutch artist Piet Mondriaan refused to paint any more flowers.[1]

Selling naturalist paintings signed with his Dutch last name had been a means of survival before his more radical work received proper recognition. "Painting flowers has nothing to do with my art. P. Mondriaan and P. Mondrian are two different people,"[2] he wrote in a letter to Theo van Doesburg, the self-proclaimed leader of the De Stijl art movement. Mondrian found the color green particularly irritating. In fact, by 1921, he had banned green from the palette of the works he considered to be his true art.

A big part of this was dramatics, and Mondrian did not shy away from repeatedly expressing his dislike for anything green. Friends and acquaintances recount how, at social gatherings, he would frequently change places at the table in order not to face the trees.[3] He always had a vase with a tulip in his Parisian studio, famously photographed by André Kertész.[4] Yet the flower was artificial, and Mondrian had painted its stem and leaves white.[5] "Too many trees," he famously blurted out when looking out of the window of his London studio in 1938.[6]

→ Fig. 11

Paradoxically, Mondrian had developed a fascination with trees during his earlier phase of landscape painting. It is through works like *Willow Grove*, *Red Tree*, *Gray Tree*, *Flowering Apple Tree*, and *Composition* that he explored a trajectory from naturalist painting to Impressionism, Cubism, and eventually pure abstraction. Gradients, transitions, twisted branches, and porous structures gradually became more abstract, rational, and thus more modern and expressive. The industrialization, modernization, and technological progress that had been gathering speed since the 1800s can here be seen as an energy that permeated all aspects of life, including art.

Trees were not still lifes but mere instruments in a search of the pure plastic expression of an immutable truth. The compositions and rhythms of lines and colors were the fundamental painted manifestation of total universal space. “Whatever is capricious and twisted in nature” was a distraction.[7] The mutable destroyed any possibility of equilibrium.

Searching for Harmony Within Infinity

This kind of analytical, abstract, and rational approach would later be used as the guiding principles of modern urban planning and design. Another Dutchman, Jaap Bakema, championed the translation of the De Stijl legacy into urban design after 1945. He built on the heritage of the diagrammatic design and programmatic organization of Dutch functionalism by deriving notions of composition and continuity of spatial elements from the elementary language of the planes, lines, and color of neoplasticist works. This play of lines and planes reproduced across scales was based on the articulation of an interrelated continuum of built elements.[8]

As with Mondrian, Bakema was searching for some form of universal order that could help people become aware of the greater context of life.

He called it a "total space [...] in which everything is and will be."[9]

→ Fig. 12

One can easily interpret much of modernist urban planning and design as being the result of an abstract, plastic search for greater clarity and order. Vice versa, one could recognize the representation of modern transportation systems, organizing elements of a rational and functional arrangement of urban blocks, neighborhoods, districts, cities, and landscapes in Mondrian's black lines—plastic compositions as plans; plans as plastic compositions. It is not surprising that Mondrian and Bakema both drew from cosmology and religion to find "harmony with infinity".[10] God's view was the view of the plan.

The ideas of modernism were pervasive, shaping cities all around the globe under the precepts of functional zoning and private mobility. Modernism appealed to governments on all political sides of the spectrum due to its efficiency in dealing with the challenges of dwelling, infrastructure, and the economy. Modern planning and design often sought total, absolute solutions. Nature (including human nature) was imperfect and needed to (and could) be controlled. Such promises infused the post-war consumer society with optimism for widespread prosperity, individualism, and free choice, all supported by the illusion of unlimited growth.

Fig. 11 An artificial tulip painted white in Piet Mondrian's studio exemplifies modern anxieties about the volatility of nature. André Kertész, *Chez Mondrian,* Paris (1926). © Centre Pompidou, MNAM-CCI, Dist. GrandPalaisRmn / Adam Rzepka.

Fig. 12 Jaap Bakema's diagram of transitional elements (1964) expresses the search for a way to articulate the relationship of people with a greater universal order across scales. Collection Nieuwe Instituut / J.B. Bakema archive, inv. nr. BAKE t42.

Recentering the Human Experience

In 1940, Mondrian arrived in Manhattan. With little green in the concrete jungle, he must have felt relief while looking at East 59th Street from the window of his studio. Mondrian loved New York—its vitality, nightlife, and dancing to boogie-woogie music. As a result of his encounters with the landscape of the modern metropolis, his work also changed.[11] His compulsiveness about the height, thickness, and composition of black-lined grids vanished. He began to experiment with colored pieces of tape in a playful and intuitive way. The Dutchman abandoned his search for universal totalities and focused on the process, on the discovery of a world with more nuances, subtler transitions, diversity, movement, and structure, all at once. In *Victory Boogie Woogie*, the city is alive and full of rhythm. By rotating the painting 45 degrees, a different perspective of the city emerges, one of infinite life and potential. There may even be open spaces—some beyond our canvas field of vision—awaiting a yet unknown filling between the colorful parts.

→ Fig. 13

Victory Boogie Woogie would be Mondrian's last painting, and it remained unfinished. We do not know whether green-colored tape was supposed to have reached it. Mondrian's celebration of urbanity would remain unnoticed by mainstream urban planning and design for quite some time to come. In fact, in the decades that followed, the mandate for urban renewal went on to raze entire neighborhoods. Under the guise of addressing urban crises and decay, planners often dismantled entire social ecologies for the sake of an efficient flow of vehicles and the economy. From New York to Rotterdam, the black lines of the traffic machine fragmented urban landscapes worldwide.[12]

→ Fig. 14

In 1961, Jane Jacobs rebelled against the rational and comprehensive approach dominating modern urban planning. In her book *The Death and Life of Great American Cities*, she argues that plans envisioned from the top down jeopardized informal socio-spatial dynamics and their ability to generate beauty and value. Social and urban fabrics are interrelated in an "organized complexity", forming an "organic whole": while streets are the main theatres of social interaction, mixed-use, historic preservation, human scale, and high density are necessary conditions enabling vitality and diversity—that is, defining great cities.

Jacobs argued that vibrant, safe neighborhoods thrive on a mix of functions, diverse buildings, and active streets. She believed that densely populated areas with varied uses and a diverse population are crucial for community vitality. Jacobs introduced the concept of "eyes on the street", where constant activity and different purposes create natural oversight and foster social cohesion. She advocated for short, interconnected blocks, mixed-use developments, and a variety of building types to encourage social interaction and community-building. Criticizing rigid government plans, Jacobs championed a more organic, community-driven approach to urban development, emphasizing that spontaneous interactions and resident involvement are key to flourishing neighborhoods.

Overall, the definition of a good city is, for Jacobs, context-specific: "One kind of city is not the destiny of our planet". Thus, the urban designer must embrace a "web way of thinking", dealing simultaneously with a great number of dynamically interconnected and rapidly changing social and spatial factors.[13] The rising concern about this loss of urbanity was adopted by authors like Manuel Castells in *The Urban Question*.[14] Jacobs and Castells' criticism of post-war urban politics highlights that the complexity of urbanity is a primary condition for a thriving urban society and a good life. In many respects, like Jacobs' city, the city of *Victory Boogie Woogie* was perhaps never meant to be finished.[15] In the decades that followed, municipal governments and their planning departments began pursuing an *urban renaissance*, creating new forms of urban mix in cities.[16] Nevertheless, the basic principles of most of these interventions were still rooted in the paradigm of modernist city planning, which puts logistics and the economy first—and only once that was arranged, could any social and ecological aspects be added. Due to a dearth of interdisciplinary development planning, new neighborhoods and districts were built with the efficiency of a housing plan and based on generic building stock. Contractors and developers were able to build quickly, even factory-like. Neighborhoods and districts emerged that were not well connected to social and ecological systems. Indeed, the landscape was still considered as being something to control and transform in support of the urbanization process.

Such a rational, efficient, and logistical approach is now deeply rooted in our DNA as urban designers. For example, the street, the most basic typology of public space, often ends up becoming a road. Handbooks and manuals for street and public space design generally omit the subsurface.[17] After the tram lines, car lanes, parking lots, separate bicycle paths and walkways, tubes, and pipes, there is often only a few spots left over for greenery and quality of stay. The street is a stretched bundle of lines that forms a barrier for people—and for other species—both above and below the ground.

Fig. 13 New York is a city alive in diversity and contingency in Piet Mondrian's *Victory Boogie Woogie* (1944). Kunstmuseum Den Haag / Public domain.

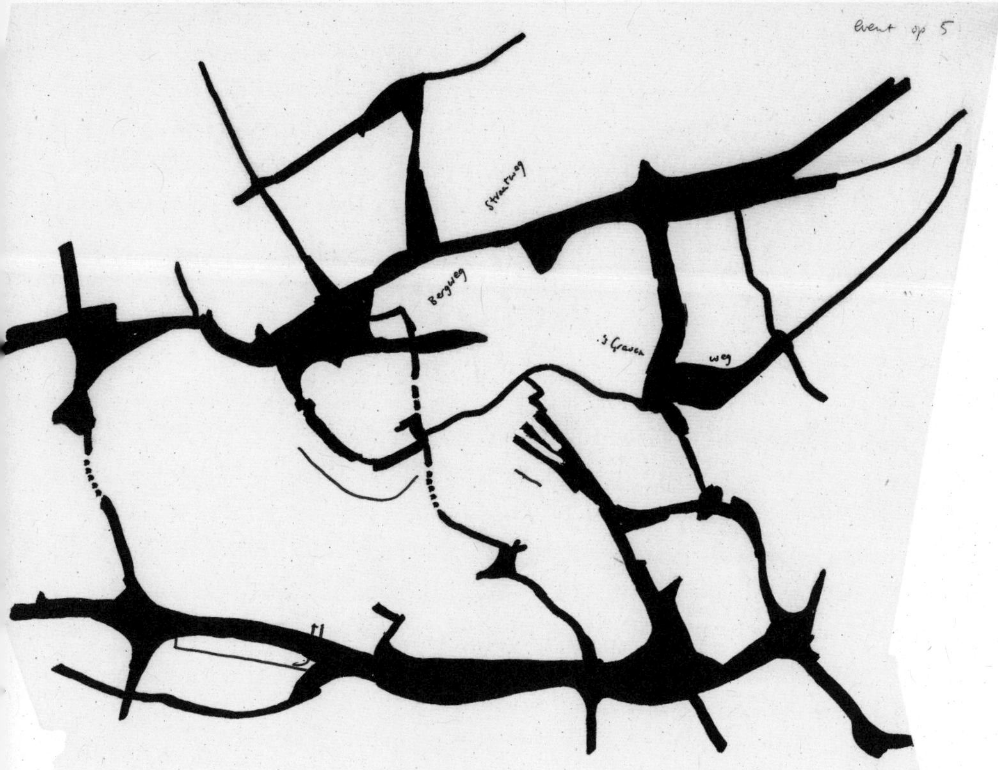

Fig. 14 Frits Palmboom's study of Rotterdam's traffic infrastructure (1985) shows the fragmentation of the Dutch city into islands. Courtesy of Frits Palmboom.

Landscape as a Multifunctional Infrastructure

Over time, Bakema and many other modernists realized that the dogmatism of modern urban planning and design was not adequately able to express the complexity of human associations. Theoretical notions of habitat and ecology became central. Instead of separating functions, communities were organized according to complexity along a "scale of association". Like in a big family, it was about being together with differences. The way these ideas about habitat entered into urban planning was far from what we might expect from our contemporary viewpoint, especially on a large scale. The city, an interconnected totality of human habitation, translated into abstractions of an almost cosmological dimension that stood in opposition to the natural landscape.

Bakema's first design for Tanthof, a new neighborhood in the city of Delft, fit in well with that paradigm.[18] The plan, drafted in 1969, followed a megastructure approach that transformed the polder landscape into a vast complex of interconnected housing nodes without any consideration for the natural context in which it was embedded. If projects for urban renewal dismantled social ecologies in the consolidated city, expansion plans like the one for Tanthof would do the same to existing natural systems and more-than-human ecologies on "empty" land.

→ Fig. 15

By that time, books like *Silent Spring*[19] (arguably the counterpart in environmental thinking to Jacobs' *Death and Life*) had inspired a new generation of grassroots environmental activists.[20] Indeed, local groups criticized Bakema's plan to the point that the city asked for a new proposal more attuned to the context and ecology of the place. The new plan, the result of interdisciplinary collaboration, took existing landscape lines as a basis for its construction, respecting existing structures and farms. Car traffic was deprioritized in favor of pedestrian and bicycle networks; waterways and landscape features formed another network, and were designed to address social and ecological concerns; finally, sub-neighborhoods highlighted a diversity of types and forms. In contrast to the precise lines drawn in black ink of the initial Tanthof plan, the playful use of thick colored markers and wobbly lines and fillings in Bakema's second sketch emphasize diversity and contingency—an *Ecological Boogie Woogie*.

→ Fig. 16 → Fig. 17

What preceded is just one possible way of telling the story of how our understanding of cities and nature has changed. These are just fragments of a much more complex, nuanced, and kaleidoscopic history of modern urban planning and design, its discontents and critiques. Even so, the realization by Mondrian, Jacobs, and Bakema that things can be done in a different way strongly captures the sense of curiosity, discovery, and possibility that is truly inspirational in the search for more livable futures. They put forward questions that are still open and which we still need to address today.

For most of this story, urban planners and designers regarded nature as something to be dominated and reshaped. Today, we recognize the potential of landscape in urban areas to perform as a multifunctional infrastructure. Landscape can play not just a decisive role in coping with the extreme events of climate change, but also support public health, and new urban circular economies. Specifically, that could mean that the urban landscape itself becomes a provider of ecosystem services, biobased materials, and related forms of socially inclusive work and infrastructure that are better suited to the scale of local communities.

A new ecological and circular economy could rise up, bred and fed by robust landscape carriers within the city.

Following calls by policy and citizens to reclaim space for nature, biodiversity, and green-blue networks, urban design has a critical role in contributing to rethinking how landscape entangles in productive and ethical ways with urban development. In the end, the transition to a socio-ecological city will only be successful if it is accompanied by a transition to an economy that is more focused on nature, the landscape, the climate, and people. In that sense, a project of deep conviviality between the social and the ecological requires a new kind of urban configuration, and challenges understandings of economic value and skills deeply entrenched in the current model of economic growth.[21]

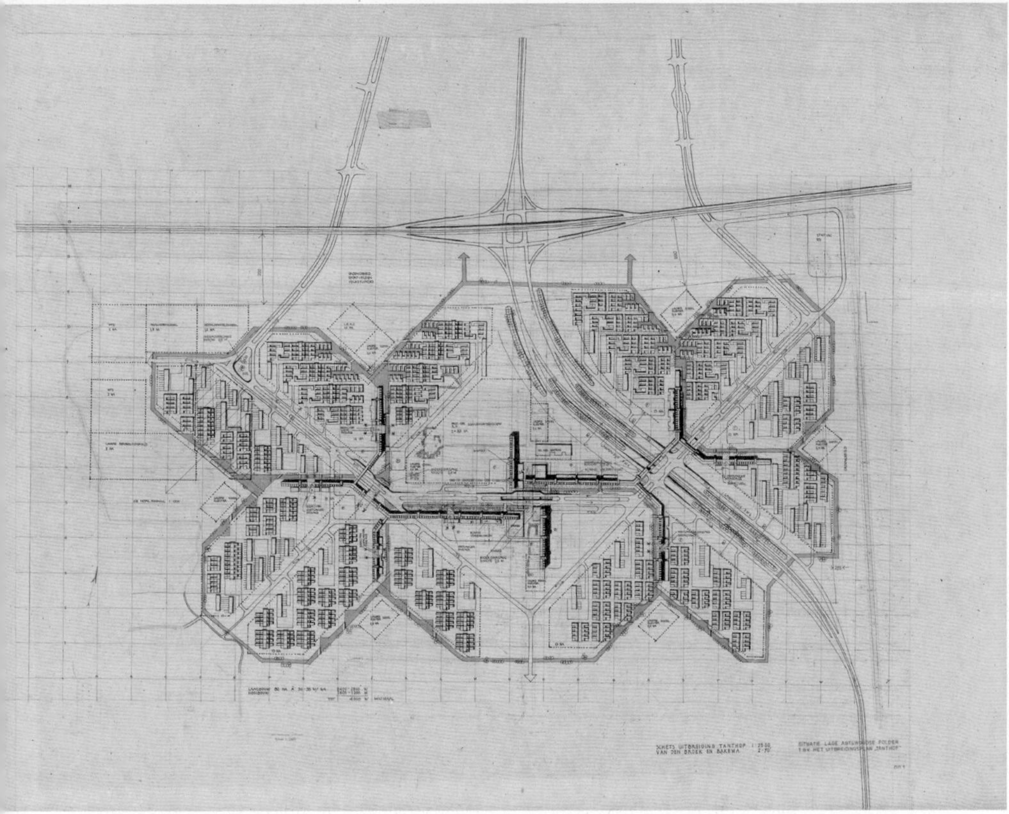

Fig. 15 Van den Broek and Bakema's first version of their urban plan for Tanthof, Delft (1969), imposed a megastructure on the polder landscape that was indifferent to the natural context. Collection Nieuwe Instituut / Architectenbureau Van den Broek en Bakema archive, inv. nr. BROX 1628r3-2.

Fig. 16 In the density studies for the second version of Tanthof, Delft (c. 1970), Jaap Bakema embraces the underlying landscapes structures. Collection Nieuwe Instituut / Architectenbureau Van den Broek en Bakema archive, inv. nr. BROX 1628 t3961-10.

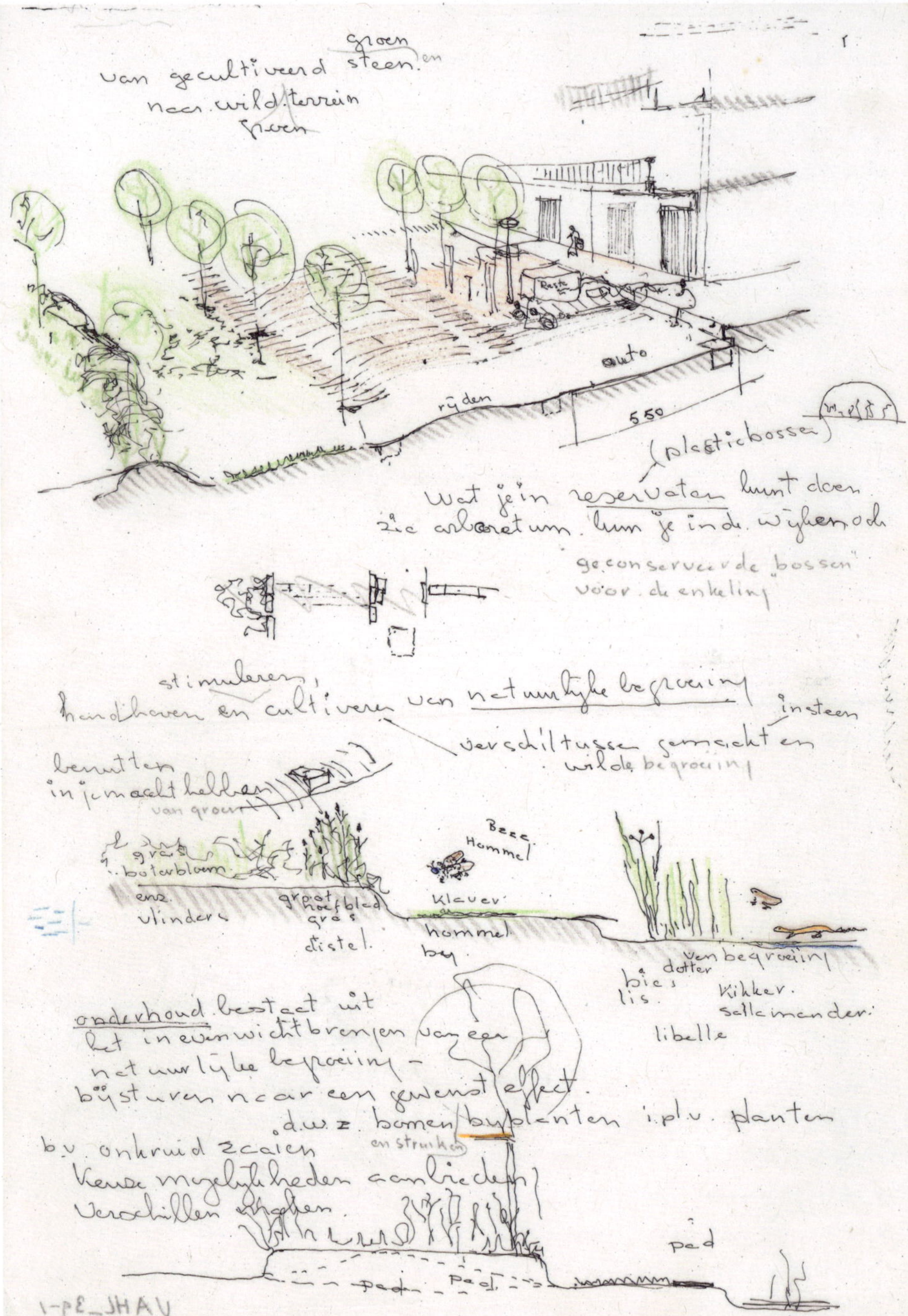

Fig. 17 Joost Váhl's sketches and notes highlight a shift in the relationship between city and landscape in the plan for Tanthof, Delft, (ca. 1970). Collection Nieuwe Instituut / Vahl, H. G. (Joost) archive, inv. nr. VAHL 39–1.

1 Michel Seuphor, *Piet Mondrian: Life and Work* (New York: H. N. Abrams, 1956), 160.

2 Alex Rutten, "Steun, weerklank en vriendschap. Over sociaal kapitaal en de breuk tussen Piet Mondriaan en Theo van Doesburg", *TS. Tijdschrift voor tijdschrift-studies* (2012): 173, https://www.dbnl.org/tekst/_tst001201201_01/_tst001201201_01_0022.php.

3 Seuphor, *Piet Mondrian: Life and Work*.

4 "Chez Mondrian, Paris", The J. Paul Getty Museum, accessed 2 August 2024, https://www.getty.edu/art/collection/object/104EKQ.

5 Seuphor, *Piet Mondrian: Life and Work*.

6 Charles Darwent, "Off the Grid—The Side of Mondrian You've Never Seen Before", *Apollo*, 30 May 2022, https://www.apollo-magazine.com/piet-mondrian-150-years-on/.

7 Piet Mondrian, "Neo-Plasticism: The General Principle of Plastic Equivalence", in *The New Art, The New Life: The Collected Writings of Piet Mondrian*, eds. Harry Holtzman and Martin S. James (Boston: G.K. Hall & Co., 1986), 132–47.

8 Dirk van den Heuvel and Víctor Muñoz Sanz, guest eds., *Total Space*, insert included in *Volume* 50 (2016); Dirk van den Heuvel, Janno Martens, and Víctor Muñoz Sanz, eds., *Habitat: Ecology Thinking in Architecture* (Rotterdam: nai010 publishers, 2020).

9 Evelien van Es, Herman van Bergeijk, and Carola Hein, eds., *Van den Broek & Bakema: Vigorous Protagonists of a Functionalist Architecture at the TH Delft* (Inaugural Speeches in the Built Environment: Global and Contextualised, no. 3) (Delft: TU Delft Open Publishing, 2018), 170.

10 Van Es, van Bergeijk, and Hein, *Van den Broek & Bakema*, 50.

11 Jürgen Stoye, "Piet Mondrian's *Victory Boogie Woogie*, 1942–44: The Painting as Illustration of the Biography of Landscape", in *Landscape Biographies*, eds. Jan Kolen, Johannes Renes, and Rita Hermans (Amsterdam: Amsterdam University Press).

12 Dutch urbanist Frits Palmboom gave this name to the modern highway infrastructures in *Rotterdam Verstedelijkt Landschap* (Rotterdam: Uitgeverij 010, 1987).

13 Jane Jacobs, *The Death and Life of Great American Cities* (New York: Random House, 1961). See also Alex Krieger, "The Kind of Problem an Urban Region Is, Early in the 21st Century", in *Harvard Design Magazine* 37 (Winter 2014): 66–73.

14 Manuel Castells, *The Urban Question: A Marxist Approach* (Cambridge, MA: MIT Press, 1977).

15 Dutch urban designer Daan Zandbelt sees this painting as a model to guide contemporary urban transformation under the premises of flexibility, diversity, mix, and inclusion. Katja van Roosmalen, "De stad als *Victory Boogie Woogie*", interview with Daan Zandbelt, Wetenschappelijk Bureau Groenlinks, 13 June 2019, https://www.wetenschappelijkbureaugroenlinks.nl/tijdschrift/zomer-2019/de-stad-als-victory-boogie-woogie.

16 Han Meyer, *City and Port: Transformation of Port Cities – London, Barcelona, New York, and Rotterdam* (Utrecht: International Books, 1999).

17 Indeed, the focus has been mostly on issues of safety, human experience, and the city at eye level. See Jan Gehl, *Cities for People* (Washington, DC: Island Press, 2010); Hans Karssenberg, Jeroen Laven, Meredith Glaser, and Mattijs van 't Hoff, eds., *The City at Eye Level: Lessons for Street Plinths*, 2nd ext. version (Utrecht: Uitgeverij Eburon, 2016). Relevant works in accounting for subsurface systems in public space design include Han Meyer, MaartenJan Hoekstra, and John Westrik, *Urbanism: Fundamentals and Prospects* (Amsterdam: Boom, 2020); and Hans de Boer, Shana Debrock, Thomas Dillon Peynado, Marleen Duflos, Mark Hendriks, Fransje Hooimeijer, Joran Kuijper, and Gijsbert Schuur, eds., *Ontwerpen Vanuit de Doorsnede: De Ondergrond als Bouwsteen voor de Toekomstbestendige Stad* (Mechelen: Public Space, 2022).

18 Extensive documentation of this case can be found in van den Heuvel, Martens, and Muñoz Sanz, *Habitat: Ecology Thinking in Architecture*.

19 Rachel Carson, *Silent Spring* (Boston: Houghton Mifflin, 2002).

20 Eliza Griswold, "How *Silent Spring* Ignited the Environmental Movement", *The New York Times Magazine*, 21 September 2012, https://www.nytimes.com/2012/09/23/magazine/how-silent-spring-ignited-the-environmental-movement.html.

21 Among other scholars, Serge Latouche argued that we need to rethink the very foundations of the idea that our societies should be based on capitalist notions of growth in *Farewell to Growth* (Cambridge: Polity, 2009).

Explore Deep Fascination

The inspirations and references from our built environment feed our design process both consciously and unconsciously. It is interesting to see for yourself how far you can stretch within it. If we share the task of designing and realizing future cities that bring about a new balance between people, nature, and the city, it can be good to have the courage to explore deep fascinations.

These can be utopias, built dream images, paintings, art, or even fairy tales. Let your fascinations sink in and try to analyze and document them in a buildable way. This is not about finding the absolute truth; stay free during this exercise and try to use your imagination in ways that might work; allow new thoughts and ideas to enrich your work and make it applicable to your own project.

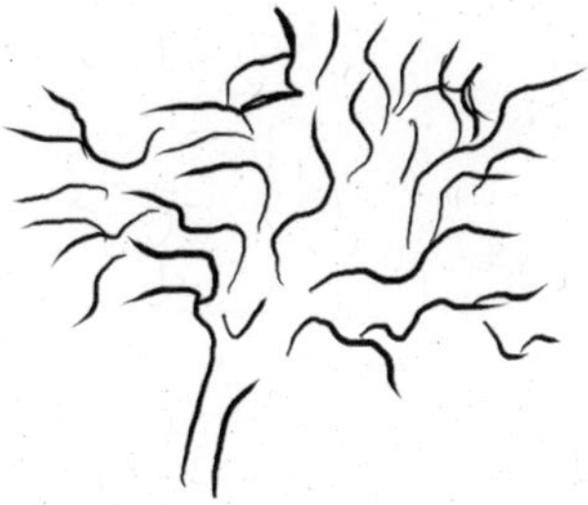

RED TREE
MONDRIAN 1908

AMSTERDAM
MEDIEVAL CENTER

BLOSSOMING APPLE TREE
MONDRIAN 1912

PLAN ZUID
BERLAGE 1915

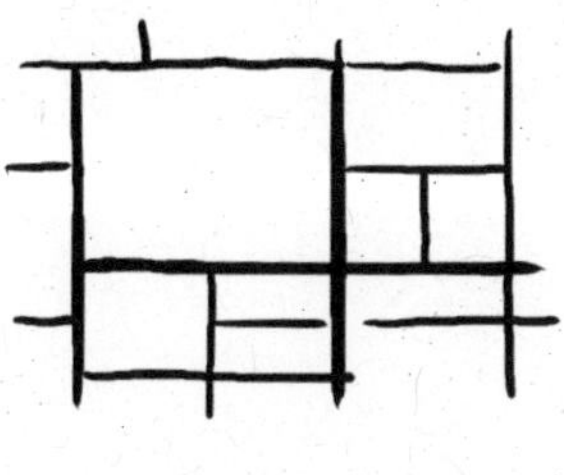

COMPOSITION
MONDRIAN 1927

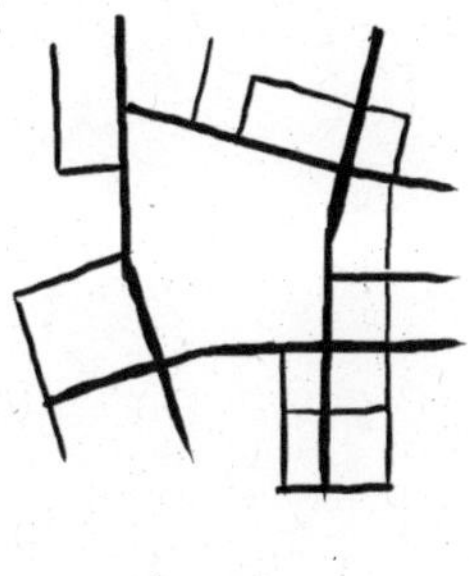

AUP
VAN EESTEREN 1934

Align and Adjust

The design workflow is a constant reiteration of, for example, context, concept, and functionality, with the aim of creating spatial character and composition. Conceptual values may arise from the (social) context in combination with inspiration from outside.

It is important to continuously anchor the concept in the context, while also zooming in and out and walking in and out. If you keep doing this repeatedly, the project will be sharpened, adapting to fit, and becoming more and more original in its environment.

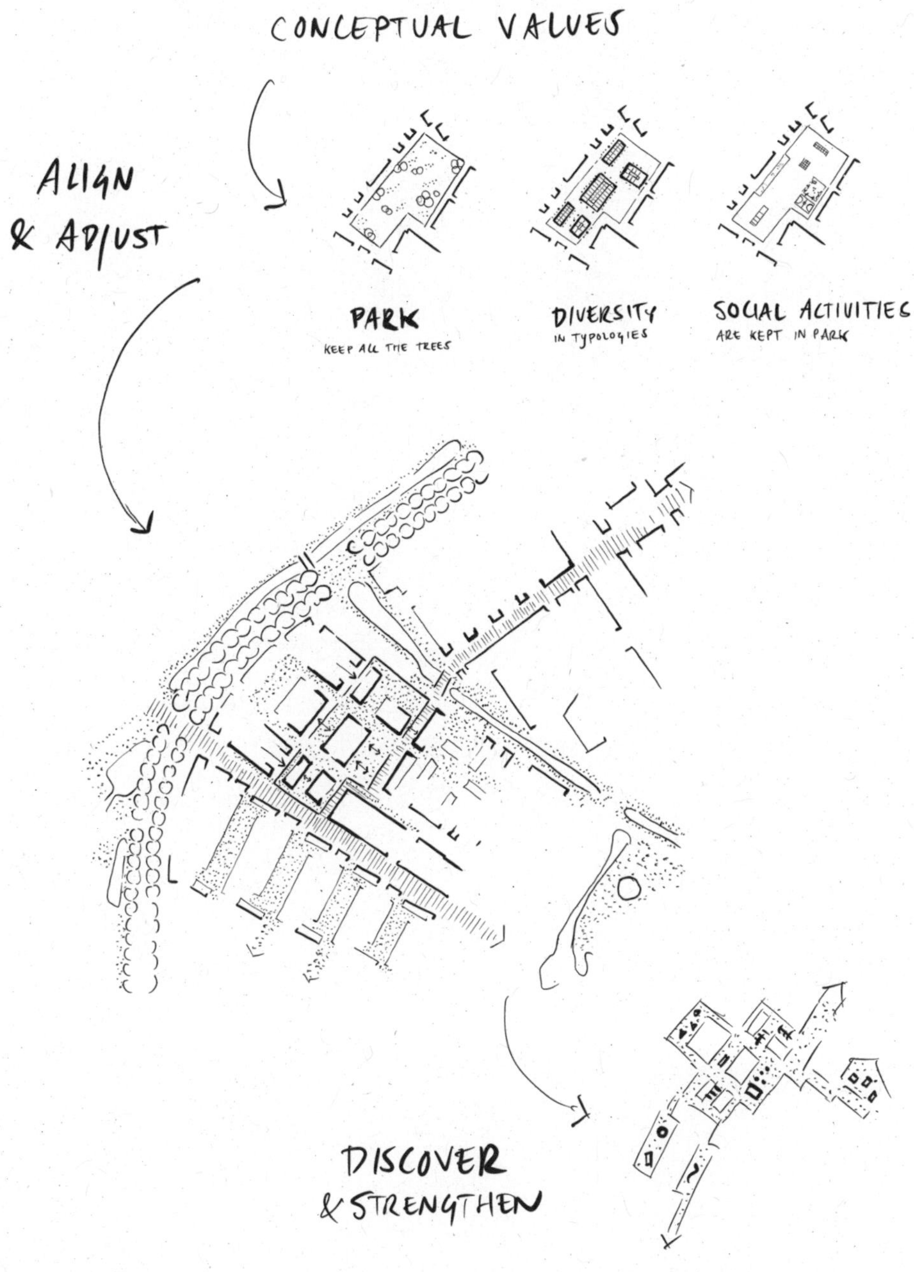
CONCEPTUAL VALUES
ALIGN
& ADJUST
PARK
KEEP ALL THE TREES
DIVERSITY
IN TYPOLOGIES
SOCIAL ACTIVITIES
ARE KEPT IN PARK
DISCOVER
& STRENGTHEN

Opening the Fabric

By understanding the structure, tectonics, character, and adaptive capacity of public space and buildings, you can add unexpected possibilities to a design. The understanding enables an urban design process to emerge from the inside out. It generates ideas for urban and cultural programming at the building level, giving reason to the relationship with outdoor space.

Because of the constant iteration from the inside out and the outside in, a design will evolve and can be anchored in the bearing structures of the city. At the same time, the design will extract the maximum strength and inspiration from the existing and new buildings involved.

The open fabric generates a patchwork of private, collective, parochial, and public places in indoor and outdoor space. This could highly stimulate a surprising, inclusive, and adaptable city in the future.

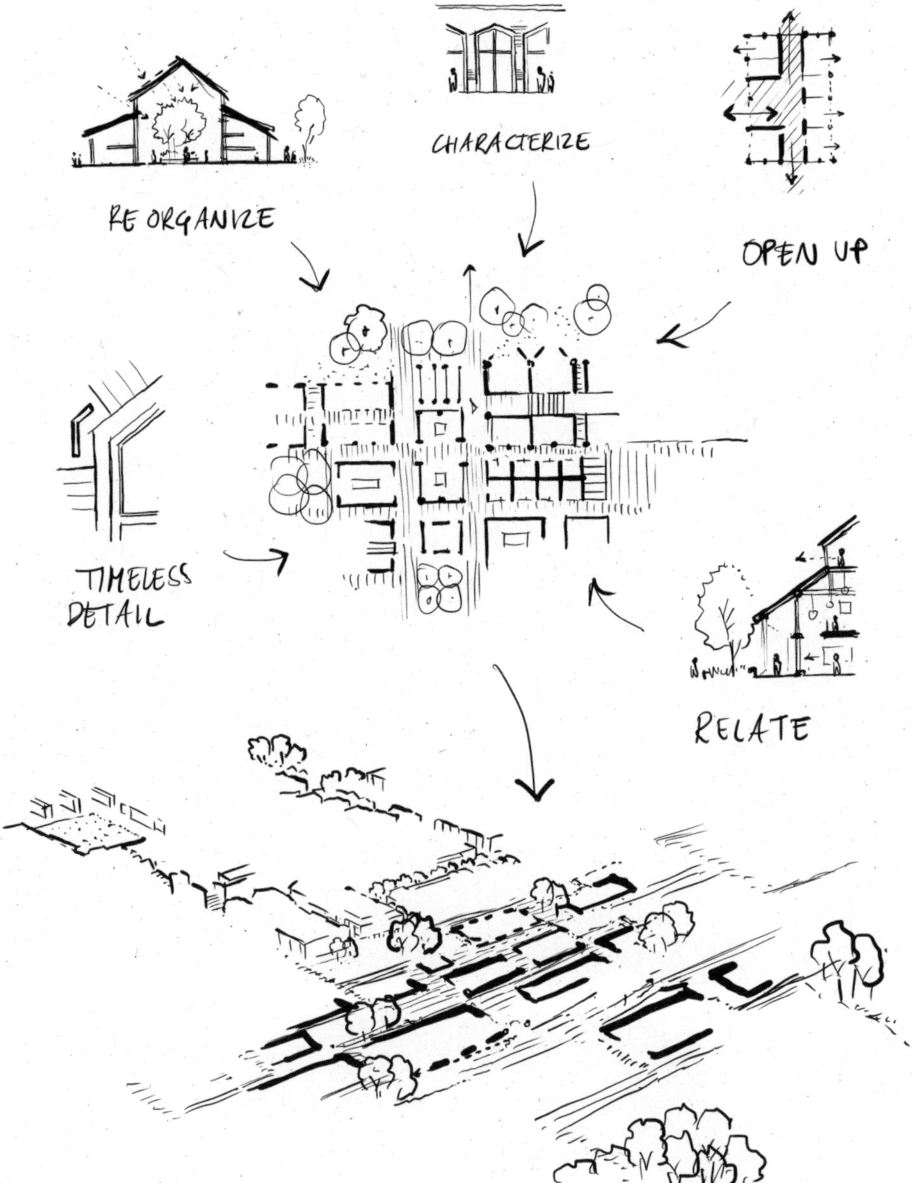
CHARACTERIZE
RE ORGANIZE
OPEN UP
TIMELESS
DETAIL
RELATE

Feedback Loops

The development of options can be seen as a constant feedback loop. By researching, analyzing, designing, and imagining the design convincingly, an iteration is created that helps you to reflect, consider, and embed. Be visionary, yet thorough, careful, and realistic at the same time.

Involve your fellow students, teachers, clients, and other stakeholders in the iteration during workshops. Inform them about the criteria you assessed the iteration with and why it is important to make strong and clear choices.

Do not forget that the urban designer is the only one who can oversee everything as a whole. You have a responsibility to be open enough to receive input, ideas, and criticism while also maintaining a strong vision and carrying the others along.

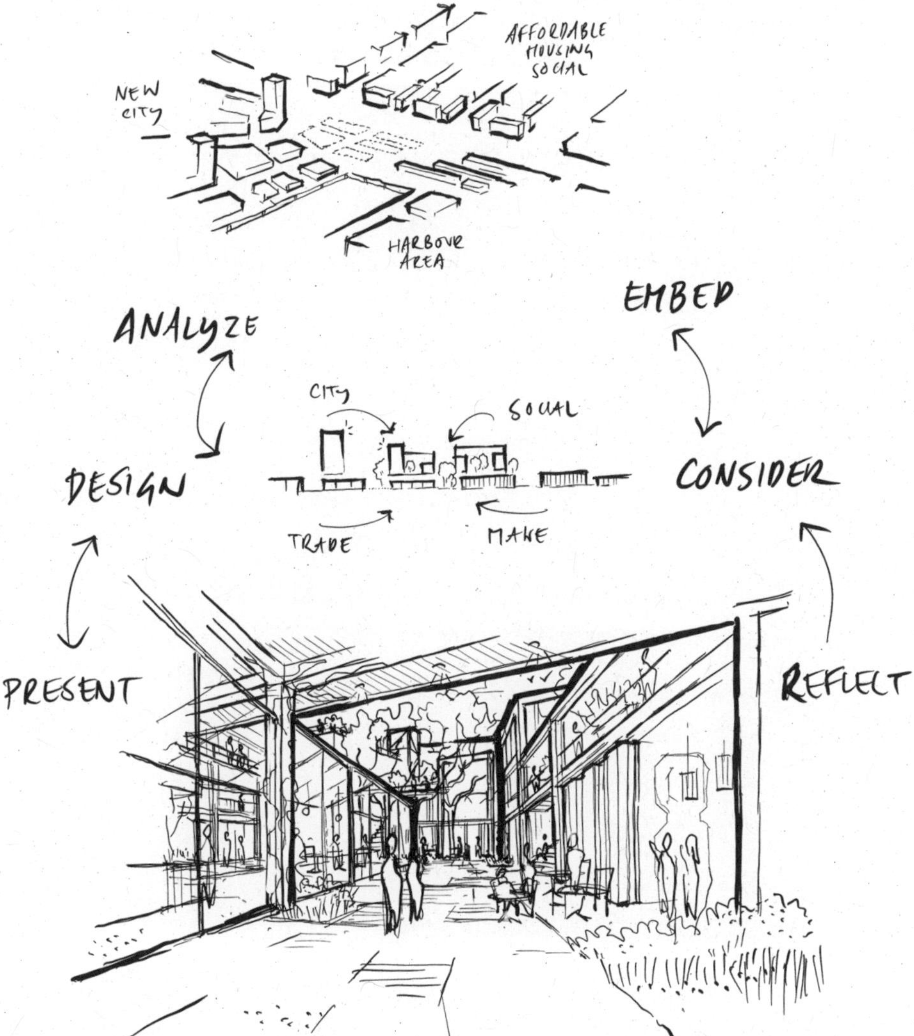
AFFORDABLE
HOUSING
SOCIAL
NEW
CITY
HARBOUR
AREA
EMBED
ANALYZE
CITY
SOCIAL
DESIGN
CONSIDER
TRADE
MAKE
PRESENT
REFLECT

Human Experience

To make a specific design more layered and more effective for the desired use, it can be interesting to conduct design research based on user experience. Talk to people and find out through in-depth interviews, surveys, and informal conversations what life is like and what their wishes and needs are. Observe the location frequently to discover patterns, activities, and situations. Document your insights in pattern maps, also analyze and sketch your new design ideas at eye level.

Be aware that users have a radius of action at different scales. This creates different patterns and insights. For example, the daily route of a child moving through the neighborhood or the way students of a dance and theater school use the outdoor space. Superimpose these patterns and insights and examine whether places should have a more exclusive character or whether opportunities for interaction and integration should arise. Keep asking yourself these questions throughout the design process. Think about who this is intended for and how interactions and multiple uses of a space and program can be beneficial for each another.

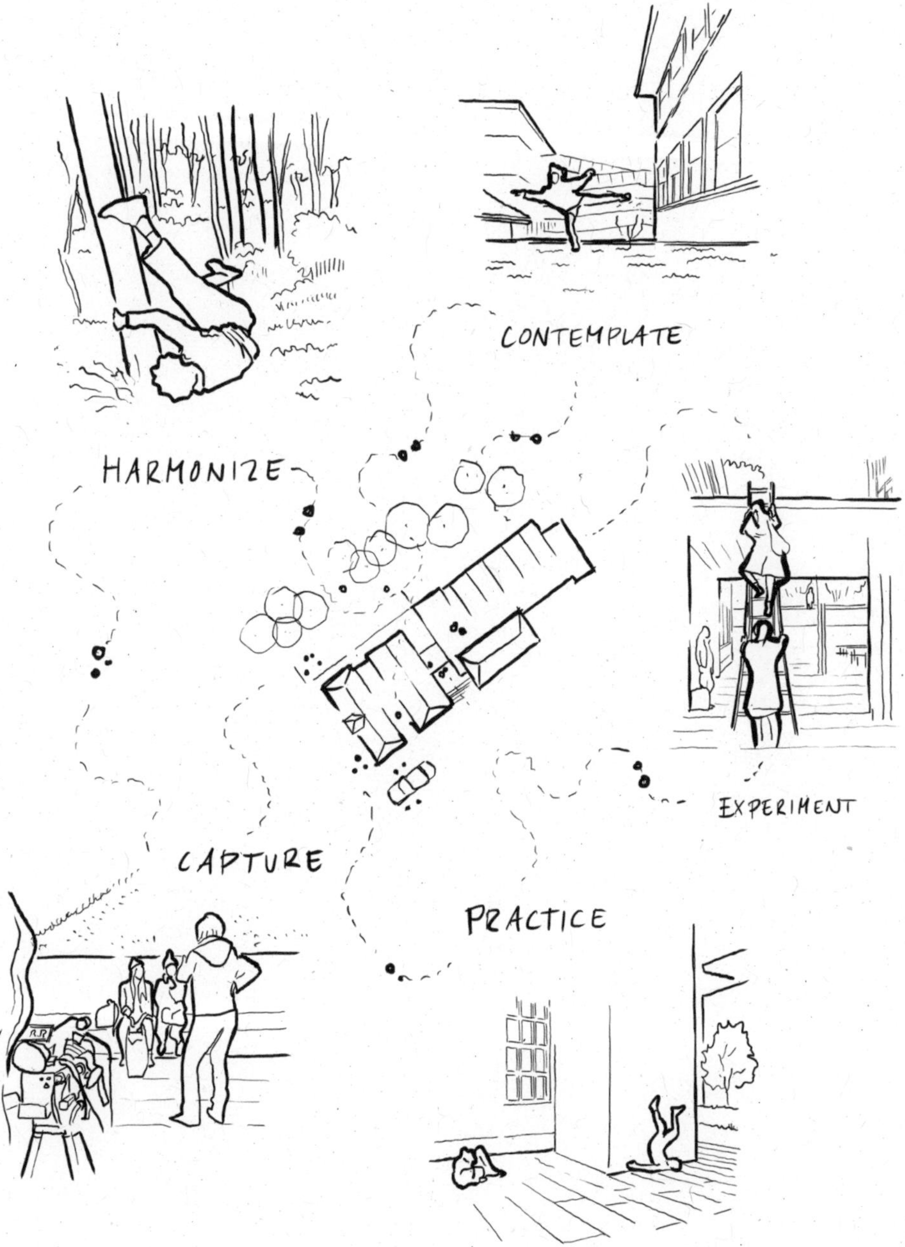
CONTEMPLATE
HARMONIZE
EXPERIMENT
CAPTURE
PRACTICE

Inter-scaling Iteration

The design process of urban design can be shaped by a constant iteration between scales. The neighborhood level is the focus, but around it we access ideas at different levels. Changes during the design process can be investigated at various scales and, together with the team, the consequences of ambitions and objectives can be assessed.

By continuing with this iteration, the right questions arise and the specialists involved can be asked. In this way, as an urban designer, you radiate that you control the project and that you are constantly giving insight into a buildable and feasible project.

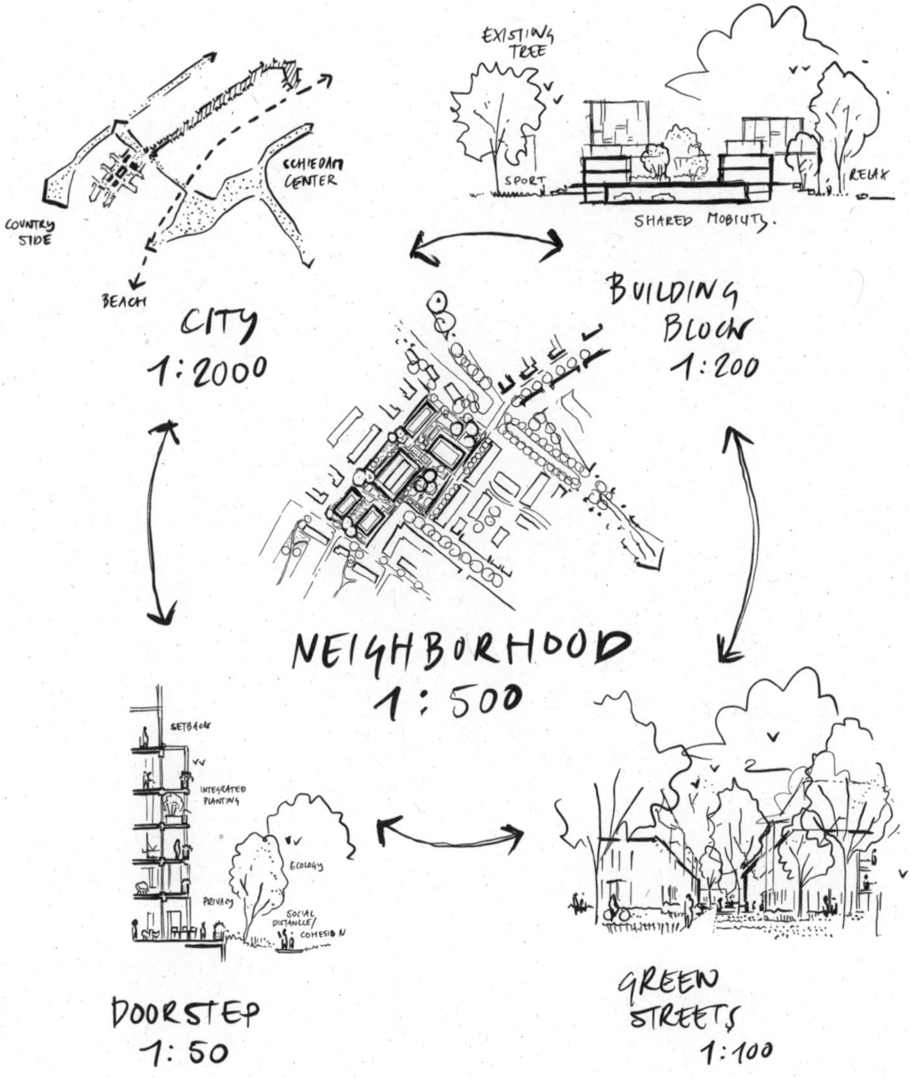
EXISTING TREE
SPORT
RELAX
SHARED MOBILITY
SCHIEDAM CENTER
COUNTRY SIDE
BEACH
CITY
1:2000
BUILDING BLOCK
1:200
NEIGHBORHOOD
1:500
SETBACK
INTEGRATED PLANTING
ECOLOGY
PRIVACY
SOCIAL DISTANCE/
COHESION
DOORSTEP
1:50
GREEN STREETS
1:100

Change in Urban Design Must Come from Within

Embracing the Tree

For many urban dwellers, the identity of a city is shaped largely by its buildings—houses, façades, iconic structures, or neighborhood styles. But as thinkers like Donna Haraway and Bruno Latour state, to truly respond to the ongoing poly-crisis, we must deeply engage with the Earth and its systems. The future identity of our living environments must be shaped to a much greater degree by landscapes and outdoor spaces. Architecture and urban design have the capacity to play a decisive role in this shift, with built forms serving as cohesive backdrops, creating frameworks that foster situations and conditions in which people can care for and identify with an expanded idea of home and community.

The act of embracing trees and other living beings, just as we do ourselves and our loved ones, offers valuable lessons in coexistence and community. Italian botanist Stefano Mancuso, for example, challenges the traditional view of trees as being passive. He argues that trees and forests provide insight on designing cities and political systems that helps foster social and ecological harmony. To build such cities, we must learn from the complexity and intelligence of the plant world. This raises an important question: What can we learn from nature, and how can these lessons reshape our relationships with the natural world, ourselves, and each other?

Unlike animals that have centralized systems, trees function in decentralized yet interconnected modular structures. Their repeated fundamental units work cooperatively, allowing them to thrive and adapt in ways quite different from animals. Trees form symbiotic relationships with fungi through the “Wood Wide Web”, an underground network that allows them to exchange nutrients, water, and information. For instance, when one tree is attacked by insects, it releases chemicals to warn its neighbors. Trees adjust growth and share resources as a community, based on available light, space, and nutrients, with older trees often protecting younger ones.

The structure of trees reveals even more wonders. Their porous leaves, trunks, and roots enable photosynthesis and store sugars for winter survival. Illustrations by Kutschera and Lichtenegger show how roots, crowns, and veins grow in constant pursuit of sunlight, water, minerals, and space. This cycle of withering and regeneration is a self-sustaining, efficient system that can serve as an inspiration for how we design cities.

→ Fig. 18

Cities, like trees, are slow to change, but unlike trees, they rely heavily on external resources. The current challenge is to design regions, cities, and neighborhoods that operate more like plants—creating sustainable, nourishing environments. Layers of urban rootscapes form a palimpsest, with elements that need to be either preserved or transformed. Many aspects of our urban heritage must be rethought in order to support deep conviviality, such as fossil-fueled mobility, rigid planning, and public spaces built on limited ecological principles. Public spaces must now mediate between social and ecological needs, reconciling urban heritage with much-needed transformations.

In the end, if we want to effectively kickstart social and ecological transitioning from within cities, we must ask the following question: Where can we find the space to transform the city into a well-connected network of solid elements, with greenspaces that have ample room to flourish, are large enough to be continuous, have ecological significance, and also provide enough space for (social) community programs, thus helping to shape the new circular economy? Given the heavy pressure on current buildings (housing crisis, but also private ownership), we inevitably need to turn to public spaces.

In fact, much of the work that needs to be done in our cities is about undoing the painful heritage of fossil-fueled mobility. The transition to sustainable mobility, traffic, and infrastructure presents a huge opportunity. The portion of asphalt in a city (around 40 percent in North American cities[1]) is jaw dropping. Vehicle infrastructure covers areas as wide as 50 to 70 meters on urban highways, expanding in some cases up to 150 meters. These vast areas act like arteries running throughout the city, with branches leading to districts, neighborhoods, and local streets. A redesign of this system could resemble a rooted structure with solid trunks and branches.

The mobility transition is moving rapidly. The share of electric vehicles to fossil fuel-powered ones has been growing in recent years, along with a rise in shared and soft mobility, expanding metro and light rail systems, and the advancement of rail travel. If we assume that this transition continues, it is reasonable to predict that in 30 years, mobility and the ways we use space will look completely different. By taking the potential for smaller and lighter vehicles (scooters, bikes) into consideration, it becomes possible to rethink the extensive infrastructure networks in cities. New infrastructures could have a sandy foundation, which would provide an environment within which ecological systems, forests, and parks could take root, creating a productive interplay with existing greenspaces and supporting different flora and fauna with the varying soil conditions.

This new green network would not only provide space for a sustainable landscape, it would still accommodate narrower, slower traffic lanes. It would create the framework and space for socially driven, circular economies to grow and flourish, fueled by the contribution and engagement of local residents, entrepreneurs, initiatives, and community organizations.

Designing cities as complex, interconnected systems—with flexible spaces and transitions—moves us away from the notion of cities as isolated parts with rigid boundaries. We could instead create dynamic environments that encourage material exchange and mutual growth. Imagine urban structures that generate and store energy, adapt to adversity, and flourish in times of prosperity—just like trees. To build positive feedback loops within cities, we need a built environment that fosters interaction, bringing people into meaningful contact with one another.

Nature's structures continue to inspire us. By seeing the city as an ecosystem, we can design it as a living organism at various scales. In organisms, spaces like contact surfaces and perforated walls allow for the exchange of oxygen, nutrients, and waste. This complex, open network could inspire us to design cities that foster interaction and material flow, rather than separating functions with rigid, inflexible boundaries.

Historically, urban planning treated landscapes as something to control and transform for industrial purposes. Instead, we should view cities as living organisms. Through spatial analysis, we can uncover branching systems that influence social and ecological interactions. It is essential to view the city holistically, while also zooming in on the capillaries and veins that bring oxygen, clean water, greenery, and social interaction to streets, courtyards, and public spaces. In urban design, we have a profound responsibility to heal, nourish, and integrate cities as part of a larger social-ecological ecosystem.

Transforming Cities from the Inside Out

To drive transformation, urban designers must deepen their collaboration with other fields, not to become experts, but to lead through interdisciplinary teamwork. Large-scale projects like former port sites and industrial zones present clear planning opportunities, but within existing urban structures, smaller strategic breakthroughs can have significant impact. These opportunities are not about traditional land division, but about rethinking public space, integrating buildings with open areas, and establishing design principles that unify fragmented urban zones. Designers need to zoom in and out, constantly reevaluating systems and expanding their scope beyond traditional project boundaries.

Urban design has now become more interdisciplinary than ever, reaching deep into the “capillaries” of the city—whether tracking human movement, animal habitat, or water and air flows. The urban designer’s role is evolving and requires close collaboration with architects, landscape architects, engineers, sociologists, and traffic experts. Together, they can develop layered strategies that enhance the city from within, building on existing structures, landscapes, and social contexts.

The future brings unprecedented, complex, and interdisciplinary tasks. How do we shift from nature-based to nature-inclusive solutions that enhance urban microclimates and support the flourishing of both humans and nonhumans? How can we rethink urban design to make cities more adaptive? What can we change that will give trees and their intricate root systems the space they need? And how do we incorporate the rhythms of ecology into our urban environments? These questions present unique design challenges and require a fundamental shift in how we plan and build cities.[2] This book provides a summary of our thoughts and experiences with the goal of inspiring younger generations and bolstering confidence about the essential role of urban design in addressing these pressing issues.

Achieving this vision of urban design for deep conviviality demands a radical shift away from rigid rules and standardized norms. Urban design must also engage politically to influence the deployment of new societal agendas and technologies, such as green-blue infrastructures, decentralized energy networks, and circular resource systems. While these systems operate at broader scales, their spatial impact is at the local level, providing opportunities to rethink urban design as a whole. The challenge is to align these agendas with practical, material concerns while prioritizing deep social and ecological conviviality.

1 Andrew Logan, "Countering Climate Change with Cool Pavements", *MIT News*, 22 August 2021, https://news.mit.edu/2021/countering-climate-change-cool-pavements-0822.

2 Students have been exploring some of these questions while taking part in the educational program of the second quarter of the urbanism master at TU Delft, titled "Designing Urban Environments", and co-coordinated by Fransje Hooimeijer, Luca Iuorio, Víctor Muñoz Sanz, and Marjolein van Esch. Robbert van der Veen was one of the tutors in this course.

Letting Landscape Lead

Based upon your knowledge and understanding of social, ecological, and technical ecosystems, you are able to carry out design exercises on different scales simultaneously. You can make the ecological and social aspects a more central part of your design strategy, which may result in surprising, secure, and divergent urban forms and design principles.

This exercise may lead to a blurred distinction between public and private spaces, or a different organization of mobility. This, in turn, can raise questions about manageability, safety, and control. Discuss these questions with the stakeholders and your design team at an early stage. This will help keep the ideas alive throughout the development process and not be hindered by any possible issues.

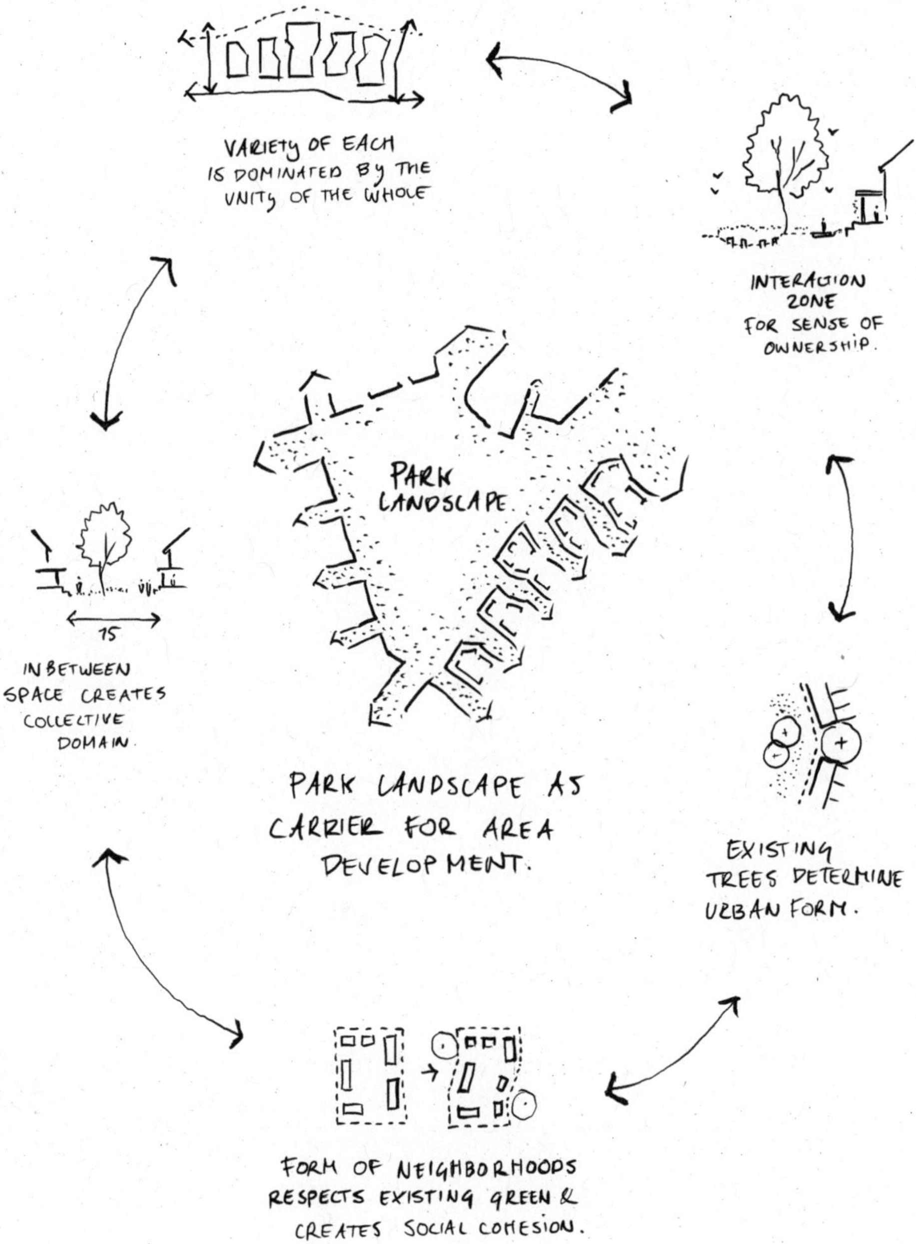
VARIETY OF EACH IS DOMINATED BY THE UNITY OF THE WHOLE
INTERACTION ZONE FOR SENSE OF OWNERSHIP.
PARK LANDSCAPE
PARK LANDSCAPE AS CARRIER FOR AREA DEVELOPMENT.
EXISTING TREES DETERMINE URBAN FORM.
FORM OF NEIGHBORHOODS RESPECTS EXISTING GREEN & CREATES SOCIAL COHESION.
15
INBETWEEN SPACE CREATES COLLECTIVE DOMAIN.

Atomize Nature

Can we design and develop regions, cities, districts, and neighborhoods by drawing inspiration from the way trees and other plants work? Can we construct evolving, sustainable structures capable of transporting materials multidirectionally, storing renewable energy, and adapting during times of adversity? What if these structures were able to flourish, grow, and evolve during periods of prosperity, driven by mutual interests and the urge to thrive?

It is awe-inspiring to think about trees, and the way they function together with the interconnectedness of the forest, as sources of inspiration. The sheer ingenuity of a tree and the inexhaustible wonders of nature are staggering. It is astonishing to comprehend how these organisms have evolved into optimal, self-sustaining systems that embody immense beauty and grandeur.

TIDAL FOREST.

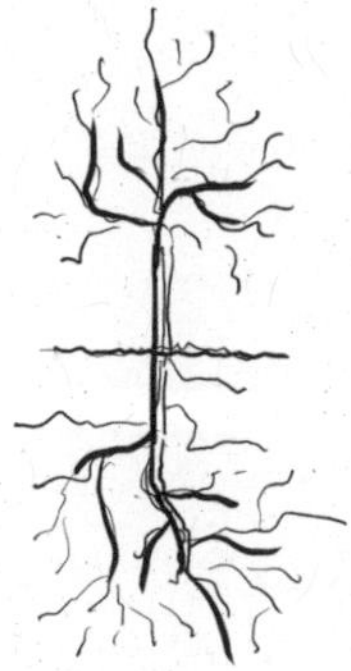

TREE

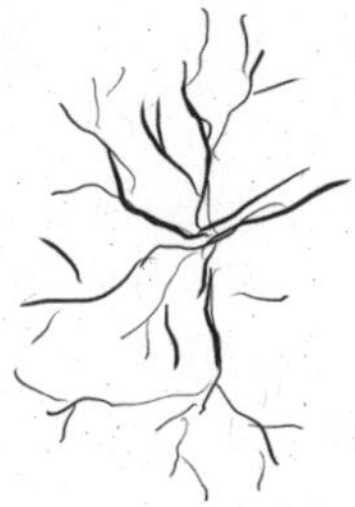

ROOT SCAPES

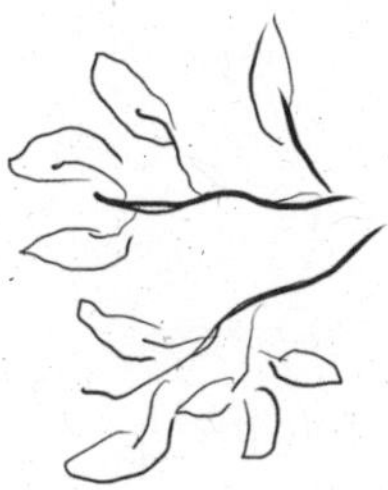

BETWEEN BRANCHES

TRUNKS

LEAVES

NERVE VESSELS

Operational Organisms

Cities can be perceived as living organisms. In a spatial analysis, we can uncover existing branching systems and further elucidate structures that influence social and ecological interactions in the city.

It is crucial to continue considering the city as a whole, while also zooming in to examine the capillaries and leaf veins that introduce oxygen, clean water, greenery, and the potential for social interaction, and community to sidewalks, private outdoor spaces, collective courtyards, and—most importantly—the public space of city streets.

Working on an urban design project gives us a significant responsibility. We can heal, strengthen, and nourish the city as a living organism. We can integrate the project as a link in the natural chain, a social and ecological ecosystem.

NETWORK GROWTH

TREE CITY

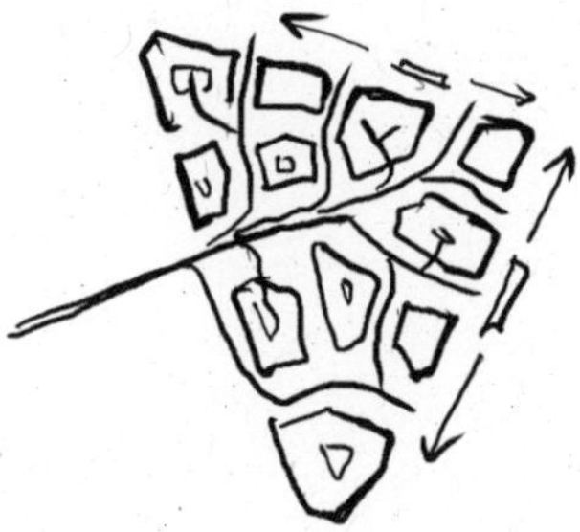

BRANCHED DISTRICT

LEAFED INTERACTIONS

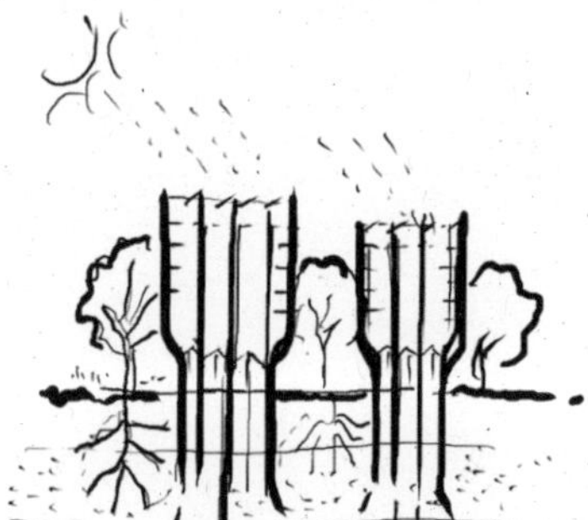

ROOTED BUILDINGS.

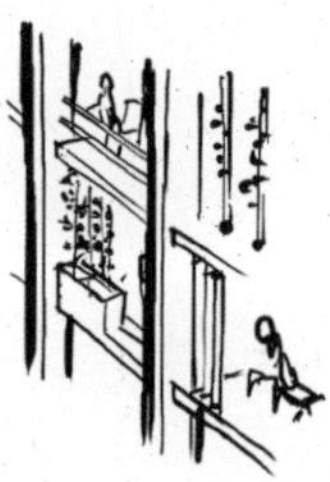

NERVED ZONES

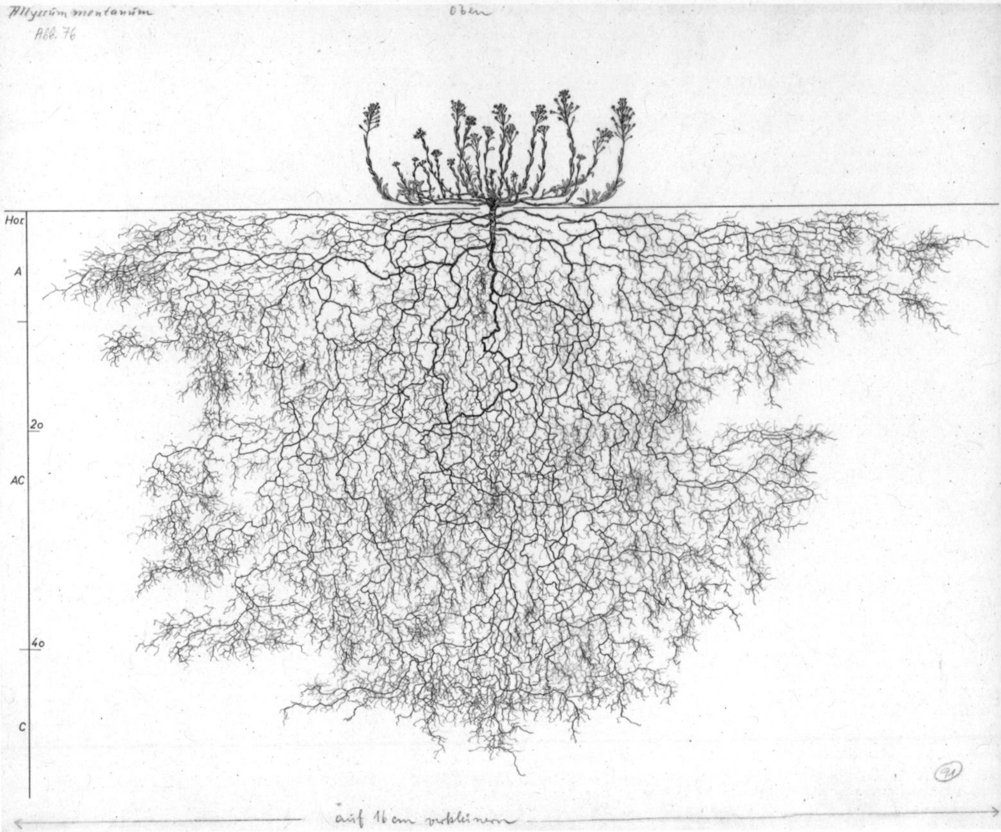

Fig. 18 This detailed drawing of an *alyssum montanum* by Erwin Lichtenegger (1992) is a celebration of the hidden root systems that ensure the growth and health of multispecies ecologies and are essential to planetary life. Courtesy of Monika Sobotik, Pflanzensoziologisches Institut.

Biotope City

The sketches in the pages that follow exemplify the practical application of the design exercises in this book in an urban environment. They aim to showcase an approach where urban spaces function as interconnected ecosystems rather than isolated entities. The goal is to create urban spaces that are both unique and unifying, with a focus on climate, social cohesion, and sustainability. The design philosophy prioritizes an understated approach to enhancing surrounding areas.

This design strategy moves away from rigid, separate city segments and promotes open frameworks with flexible transitions. This encourages ecological and economic interaction within the urban environment. The sketches illustrate the application of these principles, showing how a city can respire, engage in material exchange, and grow collectively.

The layouts incorporate green spaces, rooftop landscapes, and various meeting spots to encourage outdoor activities. The plan aims to create an open structure by integrating transportation hubs, fostering a sense of community. The focus on greenery and well-designed public spaces contributes to a comfortable urban setting suitable for diverse activities. Integrating various housing types, price ranges, and demographics is crucial for a well-rounded, mixed-use city.

City – Forest

Cities can be envisioned as an interconnected green system of linked parks and routes. By offering a fresh perspective on social and ecological aspects, projects enhance coherence among themselves while further activating the pedestrian and cycling networks in between.

District – Branches

Inspired by the metaphor of trees, branches, and leaves—as well as the power of natural systems—the plan takes shape through a branching, breathing, and open structure.

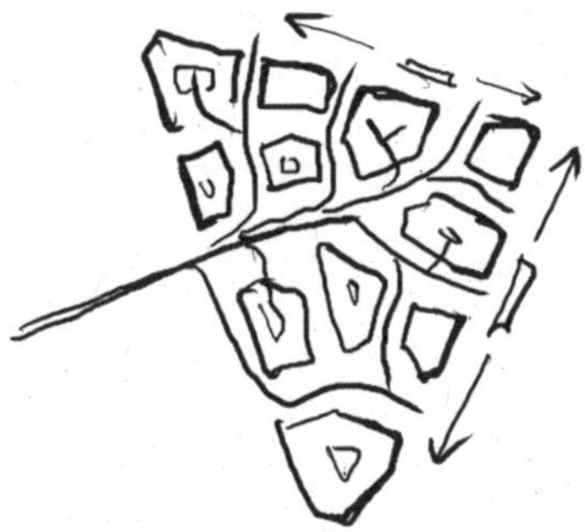

Rotated buildings create sheltered, green-filled spaces with unique identities, while the urban layout mimics branches and leaves, integrating diverse rooftop landscapes.

Branches

Leaves

This approach weaves multiple layers into a sustainable, energy-generating, and resilient system, fostering social awareness and engagement.

Flux and flow: water, people, animals

Leaves and Veins

Buildings can be envisioned as trees, drawing inspiration from their sustainable, self-sufficient systems. Rooftops are designed to harness sunlight, provide shade during hot periods, integrate green spaces for high-quality communal areas, and create a buffer for water. In the next phase, we aim to explore the potential of aquifers and geothermal energy sources.

The façades have a dual function: supporting generous outdoor spaces while remaining adaptable through flexible systems. Vertical greenery provides shade in summer, glass panels capture heat in winter, and adjustable louvers allow for precise control of incoming light and visual privacy.

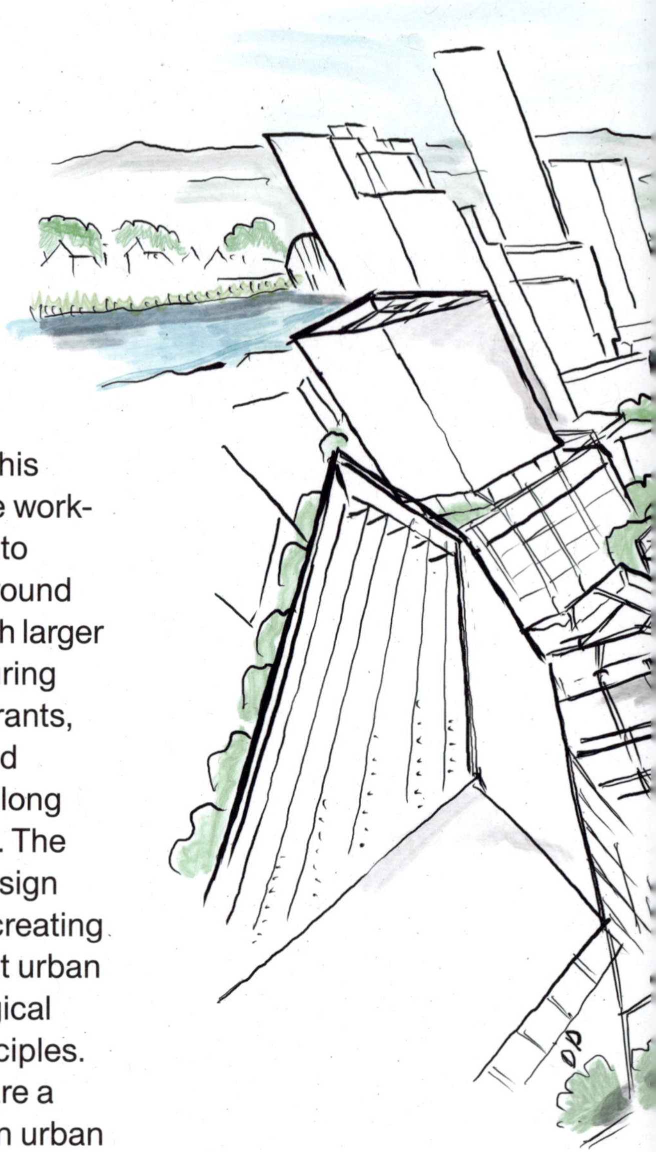

The design facilitates this integration with flexible work-spaces that can adapt to future changes. The ground floor strategy aligns with larger urban structures, featuring a mix of shops, restaurants, community spaces, and residential entrances along a branching boulevard. The sketches embody a design approach focused on creating sustainable and vibrant urban spaces through ecological and social design principles. Overall, the sketches are a final invitation to design urban areas that mirror natural processes, promoting sustainability, social interaction, community development, and environmental responsibility.

NEW SOCIAL ECOLOGICAL
LIVING ENVIRONMENT.

PLANNED DEVELOPMENT STRENGHTHENS CANYON CONCEPT
HYBRID ROOFSCAPES.

PERMEABLE
AND BREATHING
CITY QUALITY

BIKE
SHOP

CO-WORK
OFFICE

Robbert Jan van der Veen is a Dutch urban designer and co-founder of ECHO Urban Design. He works on inclusive urban landscapes from the human and social perspective. His best-known projects in the Netherlands are Herwaert Rotterdam, ZOHO Rotterdam, Esplanade Almere, and Happy Days Zoetermeer. In past years, ECHO has become established in Europe with Manufacture Lausanne, Harbour Bridge Tallinn, Leppavaraa Espoo Finland, and Limeco Limmatal Zürich. Robbert Jan holds a Master of Urban Design from TU Delft (2007, cum laude). During his studies, he co-founded an urban design firm in Rotterdam in 2006 named plein06, which grew into a multidisciplinary design office working on complex inner-city densification assignments. The company was renamed ECHO Urban Design in 2020. In parallel, Robbert Jan has been active as a design teacher at ITU (Istanbul), UVA (Amsterdam), and most recently TU Delft.

Rahul Mehrotra is the principal founder of RMA Architects. He divides his time between working in Mumbai and Boston and teaching at the Graduate School of Design at Harvard University where he is Professor of Urban Design and Planning and the John T. Dunlop Professor in Housing and Urbanization.

Víctor Muñoz Sanz is a Mexican-Spanish urban designer, researcher, and educator. Currently, he is an assistant professor of urban design at TU Delft, where he coordinates and teaches urban design studios and leads critical research on productive landscapes, urban economies, and technology. He is the author of the book *Una Rápida Compañera* (Bartlebooth 2024) and co-editor of *Automated Landscapes* (Nieuwe Instituut, 2023), *Roadside Picnics: Encounters with the Uncanny* (dpr Barcelona, 2022), and *Habitat: Ecology Thinking in Architecture* (nai010, 2022). Víctor qualified as an architect at the School of Architecture of Madrid (ETSAM, 2006) and holds a Master of Architecture in urban design, with distinction, from Harvard University Graduate School of Design (2011) and a PhD cum laude in architecture from Universidad Politécnica de Madrid (2016). In addition to his academic work, he has collaborated with offices such as Burgos & Garrido Arquitectos and Porras Lacasta in developing urban design projects like Madrid Río.

Acknowledgments and Gratitude

Although this book presents our personal reflections and positions on urban design, it could never have reached its full potential without the specific context within which it came to life. Our gratitude goes out to Robbert Jan's partner Koen de Boo and his colleagues at ECHO Urban Design, and to our fellow teachers and researchers at the Department of Urbanism at the Faculty of Architecture and the Built Environment at TU Delft. Specifically, we were crucially inspired by a series of educational and public activities held at that institution between 2022 and 2023. In these and many other related initiatives, we were never alone. We are grateful for all those whose collaboration, inspiration, feedback, and support fed into our development of the concept of deep conviviality and the writing of this book.

We would especially like to thank Rients Dijkstra and Steffen Nijhuis for their transformative discussions and collaboration on the Delft Approach and socio-ecological urbanism. We thank the entire team at the Section of Urban Design at TU Delft. Our gratitude goes out to Paulina Achurra, Verena Balz, Els Bet, Hilde Blank, Teake Bouma, Tess Broekmans, Errik Buursink, Leo van den Burg, Luisa Calabrese, Roberto Cavallo, Kees Christiaanse, Machiel van Dorst, Marjolein van Esch, Claudiu Forgaci, Milad Gholamnia, Maarten van Ham, Birgit Hausleitner, Lorena Bello, Teresa Chaparro, Maurice Harteveld, Carola Hein, Tanja Herdt, Dirk van den Heuvel, Fransje Hooimeijer, Luca Iuorio, Laura Janka, Nikos Katsikis, Wiebke Klemm, Taneha Kuzniecow Bacchin, Marco Lub, Glenn Lyppens, Janno Martens, Han Meyer, Anne Loes Nillesen, Flora Nycolaas, Sara Romero, Paulo Saldiva, Stefan van de Spek, Arjan van Timmeren, Helmut Thoele, and Daan Zanbelt.

Finally, we are deeply grateful to Hans de Boer and Jan Salden of the TU Delft Delta, Mobility, and Infrastructure Initiative for the grant that funded this publication, as well as Maarten van Ham and Joost Niermeijer, former chair and manager, respectively, of the Department of Urbanism at TU Delft, for their trust and additional financial support.

This project was supported by a generous grant from Delft Deltas, Infrastructures & Mobility Initiative of TU Delft, and the additional sponsorship of the Department of Urbanism of TU Delft.

All drawings, unless otherwise noted:
Robbert Jan van der Veen

Copy editing:
Ada St. Laurent, Vienna

Acquisitions Editors:
Baharak Tajbakhsh
Sara Lusic-Alavanja

Content Editor:
Regina Herr

Production Editor:
Amelie Solbrig

Layout, cover design and typesetting:
Bureau Sandra Doeller
(Sandra Doeller, Marcel Backscheider, Merle Petsch), Frankfurt am Main

Paper:
Vivus 100, in 120 gsm and 300 gsm

Printing:
Gutenberg Beuys Feindruckerei

Image Editing:
prints professional

RECYCLED
Paper made from recycled material
FSC www.fsc.org FSC® C009051

Library of Congress Control Number:
2025904662

Bibliographic information published by the German National Library.
The German National Library lists this publication in the Deutsche Nationalbibliografie; detailed bibliographic data is available at http://dnb.dnb.de.

ISBN 978-3-0356-2804-3
e-ISBN (PDF) 978-3-0356-2807-4

Im Westfeld 8, 4055 Basel, Switzerland
Part of Walter de Gruyter GmbH,
Berlin/Boston

9 8 7 6 5 4 3 2
www.birkhauser.com

Questions about General Product Safety Regulation
productsafety@degruyterbrill.com